AMERICAN IDIOMS AND SOME PHRASES JUST FOR FUN

AMERICAN IDIOMS AND SOME PHRASES JUST FOR FUN

AN ESL MEANING AND USAGE WORKBOOK
—contains both practice exercises and tests—

by
Edward Swick

BARRON'S

All inquiries should be addressed to:
Barron's Educational Series, Inc.
250 Wireless Boulevard
Hauppauge, New York 11788
http://www.barronseduc.com

International Standard Book No. 0-7641-0807-7

Library of Congress Catalog Card No. 98-25562

Library of Congress Cataloging-in-Publication Data
Swick, Edward.
    American idioms and some phrases just for fun / Edward Swick.
        p.   cm.
    Includes index.
    ISBN 0-7641-0807-7
    1. English language—Textbooks for foreign speakers.   2. English language—United
States—Idioms—Problems, exercises, etc.   3. English language—Terms and phrases—
Problems, exercises, etc.   4. Americanisms—Problems, exercises, etc.   I. Title.
PE1128.S977   1998
428.2'4—dc21   98-25562
                                                                    CIP

Printed in the United States of America
9 8 7 6 5 4 3 2 1

TABLE OF CONTENTS

How to Use This Book   ix

SECTION ONE Idioms and Phrases Just for Fun

Phrases Just for Fun

SECTION TWO Exercises

SECTION THREE Tests

SECTION FOUR Answers

HOW TO USE THIS BOOK

TO THE SELF-STUDY STUDENT

You will find using this book rather easy but you need to follow some simple steps in order to be successful in learning new idioms.

1. Study the meaning and usage of TEN or TWENTY IDIOMS at a time. If you need more explanation or clarification, talk to a teacher or English-speaking friend.

2. When you feel you understand the idioms, practice forming sentences with them. Use the examples in the dictionary section in the first part of the book as an aid. Do not *write* them. Do not *think* them. *Say them out loud.* Remember that language is primarily a speaking tool.

    > EXAMPLE: (Idiom 1—**about**) The sample sentence given in the dictionary section is: The film is <u>about to start</u>. You form similar sentences.

    > The class was about to end.
    > Mary was about to speak again.
    > The janitor was about to turn out the lights.

    > You can be as complicated or original as you like.

3. Write out the exercises for the idioms you have studied and practiced. Use the Answer Key at the back of the book to check your answers. You can have a teacher or English-speaking friend go over the sentences you wrote for accuracy.

4. Review the meaning and usage of the idioms for which you had errors in the written exercises.

5. Practice forming sentences with them out loud.

6. When you are certain you know the idioms well, take the appropriate test at the back of the book. You should set a goal for yourself. What is the level of accuracy you will accept as a minimum? 75%? 85%? 100%? If you do not achieve that goal, follow the earlier steps listed above, and take the test again at a later time. Use the Answer Key at the back of the book to correct your work, and have a teacher or English-speaking friend go over the original sentences you wrote.

Note that the tests come in two forms. Some are for ten idioms; others are more challenging and are for twenty idioms.

Test One—Idioms 1–10	Test Five—Idioms 61–70
Test Two—Idioms 11–30	Test Six—Idioms 71–90
Test Three—Idioms 31–40	Test Seven—Idioms 91–110
Test Four—Idioms 41–60	

After every group of ten idioms, and in a longer list at the end of the dictionary section, you will find *A Phrase Just for Fun.* You can learn these idioms by following the steps previously listed but there are no exercises or tests for these—they are "just for fun."

TO THE ESL TEACHER

Here are some helpful ideas that can make using this book more efficient for you and a success for your students. The ideas are presented as steps that can act as the guide for using the materials in the text.

1. Introduce TEN IDIOMS at a time by describing the meaning of the idiom and how it is used in English.

    EXAMPLE: (Idiom 1—**about**)
    Meaning: ready to begin an action
    Usage: followed by an infinitive

    a. Have the students pronounce the sample sentences after you:

    John's father was <u>about to</u> leave for work when the phone rang.
    The film is <u>about to</u> start.

    b. Give simple cues (which you can base on the written exercises) and have the students form new sentences with the idiom:

    Cue: He leaves for school.
    Student: He is about to leave for school.

    Cue: Tom goes home.
    Student: Tom is about to go home.

    Cue: They started the race.
    Student: They were about to start the race.

    c. Ask students to form original sentences with the target idiom.

2. When your class is using the <u>spoken</u> idioms comfortably, you can assign the appropriate written exercises. An Answer Key can be found at the back of the book. It is good practice to have students read their written work out loud. If you discover that there are errors with certain idioms in their written form, repeat Step 1 and drill the problem idioms again.

3. When you feel the students are prepared, evaluate their progress or success with the idioms by using the tests provided at the back of the book. Set a minimum goal for your students that, if not achieved, indicates that they should repeat Steps 1 and 2. You will know what percentage of accuracy is proper for your class: 75%, 85%, or 100%.

4. A culminating exercise could be the assignment of a ten- or fifteen-line dialogue, in which the students must include a different idiom in each line. For example:

> MARY: I was <u>about</u> to leave for school when I saw you here.
> TOM: I'm glad you stopped. I <u>have a bone to pick with</u> you.
> MARY: Just what are you trying <u>to get at</u>?
> TOM: I saw you with Bill yesterday. I thought you <u>were dating me</u>.

Note that the tests are provided in two forms: some evaluate ten idioms; others are more challenging and evaluate twenty idioms.

Test One—Idioms 1–10

Test Five—Idioms 61–70

Test Two—Idioms 11–30

Test Six—Idioms 71–90

Test Three—Idioms 31–40

Test Seven—Idioms 91–100

Test Four—Idioms 41–60

After every ten idioms and in a list at the end of the dictionary section, you will find some *Phrases Just for Fun*. These idioms can be drilled as described above but there are no exercises or tests for these items. They are "just for fun." These phrases and words are slang or trendy, and most provide some insight into a more current or youthful way of speaking, such as "to hang out with" or "to tick off." Some are just pat phrases that have been used in the language in a single form for decades, such as "Many happy returns of the day." They can be a lot of fun and a refreshing diversion from the regular classroom routine. They also tend to be of great interest to young people.

AMERICAN IDIOMS AND PHRASES JUST FOR FUN

1. ABOUT

You probably already know the preposition **about**, which has a meaning similar to **concerning** or **of**.

> This is a story <u>about</u> a family of lions.

It can also mean **approximately**.

> His daughter is <u>about</u> eighteen years old.

The word **about** also has a very special usage. It tells that someone or something is ready to begin an action. Note that in this usage it is followed by an infinitive.

> John's father was <u>about to leave</u> for work when the phone rang.
> The film is <u>about to start</u>.

2. ABROAD/TO GO ABROAD

This phrase says that someone is **traveling to another country**.

> Maria and John love <u>to go abroad</u>. Their favorite city is Paris.

When **abroad** is used with other verbs, it shows that **someone is located in a foreign country**.

> Her brother <u>is</u> still <u>abroad</u>.
> My parents <u>have been living abroad</u> for five years.

3. TO BE AFRAID

You already know that **to be afraid** means that someone feels **fear**. But it is also often used to show **regret**.

> I'm <u>afraid</u> I can't help you today.

4. ALL OF A SUDDEN

This phrase is similar to the more common adverb **suddenly**, and can almost always be used in place of it.

> <u>All of a sudden</u> there was a loud knocking at the door.

5. ALL OVER

This phrase is used in place of **over** when it is standing alone, and has the meaning of **ended** or **completed**.

Unfortunately, their relationship is <u>all over</u>.   (ended)
It's <u>all over</u>. We can go home now.   (completed)

6. NOT ALL THERE

This phrase says that someone is **weak-minded or somewhat unable to think clearly**. In a crueler sense it means **crazy**.

He spoke strangely. He did <u>not</u> seem to be quite <u>all there</u>.

7. TO ANSWER

This word is usually used as the opposite of **ask** or **question**. As an idiom it is used mostly in three ways:

1. Someone hears a knock at the door, goes to it, and opens it.

    It was John who <u>answered the door</u>.

2. The telephone rings, and someone picks up the receiver.

    After the third ring, Grandmother <u>answered the phone</u>.

3. The doorbell is rung, and someone opens the door.

    I'm in the shower. Someone else will have to <u>answer the bell</u>.

8. TO BE AWARE (OF)

This phrase says that the speaker **already knows about** something. Use the preposition **of** when the phrase is followed by a noun or pronoun.

Why must you remind me that it's raining? <u>I'm aware of</u> the storm.
Jim <u>wasn't aware</u> that his shoes were untied.

9. TO GET ON THE BALL

This amusing little phrase says that someone needs to **improve** something.

Your work is so sloppy. <u>Get on the ball</u>!
Tom has been too lazy. He needs <u>to get on the ball</u>.

10. TO MAKE A BEELINE FOR

Use this idiom to mean that someone is **headed directly** toward some place. It also often suggests that **speed or haste is involved**.

Jack was hungry. He <u>made a beeline for</u> the cafeteria.

A PHRASE JUST FOR FUN

ALL THAT

This is a very youthful expression to say that someone is **very good-looking**. And it can be used with either men or women.

Anna is so pretty! She's really <u>all that</u>!
Stop bragging. You're not <u>all that</u>.

---

11. ON BEHALF OF/ON SOMEONE'S BEHALF

This phrase says that someone is doing something **for** someone else or **in the place of** someone else.

Mr. Brown cannot be here tonight, so I"ll be speaking <u>on his behalf</u>.
<u>On behalf of</u> all the graduates, allow me to thank you.

12. TO BET ONE'S BOTTOM DOLLAR

Use this expression to say that you are **absolutely certain** about something, so certain that you would bet your last dollar.

I'd <u>bet my bottom dollar</u> that the Bulls will win.

13. BETTER

You know this word to be the comparative of **good** but it also has a special usage that says that someone **should** do something or **ought** to do something. It also carries with it the idea of a slight **warning**. Use it with a verb or verb phrase.

You'd <u>better</u> be careful.
My brother <u>better</u> come home on time tonight or Dad will be furious.

14. TO HAVE THE BLUES/TO BE BLUE

To many the color blue suggests coolness or calm, but in this idiom it means that someone is **sad** or **depressed**.

> Since Jane stopped dating Bob she's <u>been</u> very <u>blue</u>.
> Don't <u>be blue</u>. Think about all the happiness you've had.

15. TO HAVE A BONE TO PICK WITH SOMEONE

This strange-sounding phrase means that someone is **upset** or **angry** with someone else and wants to **discuss the problem**.

> Don't leave just yet. I still <u>have a bone to pick with</u> you.
> Mom went back to the store. She <u>has a bone to pick with</u> the clerk.

16. TO BREAK DOWN

Usually this expression is used to say that a machine has **stopped working**.

> The dishwasher <u>has broken down</u> again.

But when it is used with people, it says that someone has become very sad or upset and has **begun to cry**.

> Grandmother <u>broke down</u> upon hearing the news of the fire.
> The poor man couldn't control his tears and suddenly <u>broke down</u>.

17. TO BREAK THE ICE

This idiom really has nothing to do with ice; instead, it says that someone was the **first to approach** another person.

> The silence was long, but Maria <u>broke the ice</u> with a simple "hello."

18. A BREATH OF FRESH AIR

Use this idiom to say that a **welcome change** has taken place. The change can be a person or a situation.

> No one spoke at first, then John's little joke came as <u>a breath of fresh air</u>.
> The room was filled with napping old men. Mary's sudden appearance <u>was a breath of fresh air</u>.

19. UNDER ONE'S BREATH

This simply means **in a whisper** or **very quietly**.

"This film is so boring," he said <u>under his breath</u>.

20. TO BRUSH UP ON

This expression is used to say that someone should **study something again** or **finally learn it correctly**.

The test is tomorrow. I'd better <u>brush up on</u> the last chapter.
You had problems at the last soccer game. You need <u>to brush up on</u> your basic skills.

A PHRASE JUST FOR FUN

TO HANG OUT WITH

Don't let this unusual phrase puzzle you. It simply means **to spend time with** someone or **to go somewhere with** someone. It often means that a friendship is involved.

I like <u>hanging out with</u> Anna. She's a nice girl.
It was too hot to play ball, so Tom and I just <u>hung out with</u> one another.

---

21. TO BUTT IN

This phrase is often used in place of **to interfere**.

It's none of your business. Don't <u>butt in</u>.
We were having a quiet talk. Then Bill arrived and tried to <u>butt in</u>.

22. BY THE WAY

These three words probably don't give you a clue as to their combined meaning. This phrase is used when someone **doesn't want to forget to mention** something.

<u>By the way</u>, I saw Mrs. Brown yesterday. She looked very sick.
I'm glad that you'll be at the party tonight. And, <u>by the way</u>, I'll be there, too.

23. A CARD

This word describes a man (more rarely, a woman) who is very **funny** or **witty**.

> I like Jack. He's such <u>a card</u>.
> You always make me laugh. You're <u>a real card</u>.

24. TO CATCH (A VEHICLE)

Normally, you use this verb to say that you **captured** someone or that a **ball was involved**.

> They <u>caught</u> the robber in the basement.
> That boy never could <u>catch</u> a ball. He's just no athlete.

But it is also used to show that someone has **arrived in time to take transportation**.

> I have to go. I have <u>to catch the next bus</u>.
> Can you tell me where I can <u>catch a cab</u>?
> If you don't hurry, you won't be able <u>to catch the morning train</u>.

25. TO CATCH ON

When used with the preposition **on**, this phrase means the same thing as **understand**.

> This is a hard job, but she <u>caught on</u> fast.
> I heard the joke twice, but I just didn't <u>catch on</u>.

26. A CHIP OFF THE OLD BLOCK

This strange combination of words means only that **the son** (rarely the daughter) is very much **like the father**.

> Look at Jim's eyes and nose. He's really a <u>chip off the old block</u>.

27. A COCK-AND-BULL STORY

Use this expression to say that what someone has said is **quite unbelievable** and perhaps even **a lie**.

> He said he swam across the lake, but I think it's just a <u>cock-and-bull story</u>.

28. TO COME ACROSS AS

These words mean **to seem like**.

> She <u>came across as</u> rather stupid, but she was one of the best readers in the class.

29. TO COME TO

This phrase means that someone has **awakened**, usually from an unconscious state or after a serious illness.

> Mr. Jones was in a coma for a week. He finally <u>came to</u> this evening.
> After the accident the fireman couldn't get the injured woman <u>to come to</u>.

30. TO COME TO KNOW (SOMEONE)

This expression is used to say that you **became acquainted** with someone and had a special understanding of what that person was.

> I <u>came to know him</u> him well after a long camping trip.
> She was so quiet at first but when he <u>came to know her</u>, he discovered a very talkative girl.

A PHRASE JUST FOR FUN

HOT

You already know that this word is the opposite of **cold**. It can also suggest that someone is **sexually aroused**. However, here it means that some man or woman is **extremely good-looking**.

> Look at that boy over there! He's really <u>hot</u>!
> John continued to stare at the new girl in class. She was the <u>hottest</u> girl he had ever seen.

---

31. TO COPE WITH

This phrase means that someone is **handling a problem with difficulty**. The problem can be with a person, a thing, or a situation.

> His family had to learn <u>to cope with</u> his alcoholism.
> I just can't <u>cope with</u> John anymore. He's hopeless.

32. CUT-AND-DRIED

Use this expression when you want to say that something is **absolutely clear** to you or that **there is no questioning it**.

> There is a <u>cut-and-dried</u> solution to the problem. We have to build the dam.

33. TO CUT A CLASS

Many languages have a special verb that says that a student **intentionally misses** a class. In English the verb is **to cut**.

> John hates history. He <u>cut</u> three classes this week.

34. TO DATE (SOMEONE)

This verb says that someone is **seeing** another person **regularly**. They are becoming a couple, and their relationship is becoming **romantic**.

> Maria <u>has been dating</u> Thomas for two months already.
> I'm too busy. I don't have time <u>to date</u>.

35. TO BE UP TO DATE/OUT OF DATE

These two phrases express the ideas that someone or something is **modern** or **old-fashioned**.

> She always has the latest clothes. She's really <u>up to date</u>.
> Don't you think disco is a little <u>out of date</u>?

36. TO DIE AWAY

Use this idiom to mean **to become quieter** or **to become weaker**. The word also suggests that this happens **gradually**.

> The sound of her voice <u>died away</u> as she disappeared into the fog.

37. TO DO WITHOUT

This verb says that someone cannot **bear being without** a certain person or thing.

> I'm so depressed. I can't <u>do without</u> her.
> During the war we learned <u>to do without</u> many luxuries.

38. I WOULDN'T DREAM OF IT

The infinitive form is rarely used with this expression. It appears mostly in its conjugated form and means that someone **is certain that he or she would not do** something.

> Me? Run a marathon? <u>I wouldn't dream of it</u>!
> Jack <u>wouldn't dream of</u> going to the dance without me.

39. TO EAT ONE'S OWN WORDS

This phrase says that someone **is wrong about what he or she has said** and now **has to admit it**.

> The meteorologist promised good weather, but now <u>she's eating her own words</u>. What a storm!
> I was sure that Smith would win the election, but I suppose I'll have <u>to eat my own words</u>.

40. TO KEEP AN EYE ON

This unusual expression means that someone will **watch carefully** or **guard** something.

> <u>Keep an eye on</u> my car. I have to go to the bank.
> I can't leave right now. I want <u>to keep an eye on</u> the pot on the stove.

A PHRASE JUST FOR FUN

TO KICK THE BUCKET

This expression is usually used when someone speaks about someone else's **death** in a **casual** or even **comic** manner. Its synonym is **to die**.

> When you <u>kick the bucket</u>, you're going straight to hell.
> Her house was sold a couple of years after Granny <u>kicked the bucket</u>.

---

41. FACE TO FACE

This phrase means that two people are **together** and perhaps even **looking at one another**.

> The two leaders finally met <u>face to face</u> to discuss an end to the war.

42. TO FALL IN LOVE/TO BE IN LOVE

These idioms mean that someone is **gradually developing a romantic relationship** with another person. When the development is complete, they **are a couple**.

> I didn't want <u>to fall in love</u> with Mary, but she's so wonderful.
> My grandparents <u>have been in love</u> for fifty years.

43. IN THE FAMILY WAY

This phrase is used in the place of **pregnant** or **expecting a baby**. It can refer to the mother-to-be or to the couple.

> Anna is <u>in the family way</u> again. This is her fourth.
> They're so happy. They're finally <u>in the family way</u>.

44. TO BE FED UP WITH

This unusual combination of words says that someone is **completely annoyed with** someone or something.

> I quit! I'm <u>fed up with</u> this job.
> Mom was finally <u>fed up with</u> the behavior of her neighbor's dog and called the police.

45. TO FEEL LIKE

This phrase has nothing to do with **feelings**. It is used in place of **to wish**. Note that it is usually followed by a gerund (going, walking, buying).

> Do you <u>feel like</u> taking a walk?
> I really don't <u>feel like</u> arguing about this again.

46. TO FIRE (SOMEONE)

This verb is used to say that someone is being **discharged** or **losing his job**.

> Bill came late to work again and was <u>fired</u>.
> The boss threatened <u>to fire</u> her because of her inefficiency.

47. FISHY

This little word gives the idea that information **smells bad** and that it is probably **false** information.

> The facts in his report were rather <u>fishy</u> to everyone in class.

48. FIT AS A FIDDLE

This phrase means that someone is **in good health** or **in good physical condition**.

> She was in the hospital for two weeks, but now she's <u>fit as a fiddle</u>.
> Tom exercises every day. He's <u>fit as a fiddle</u>.

49. TO FOOT THE BILL

Use this expression to say that someone **has to pay the bill** but is probably **reluctant** to do so.

> Everyone left the restaurant in a hurry, so John was left <u>to foot the bill</u>.

50. TO GET IT

You are probably familiar with the verb **to get** and the many unusual ways it is used. Its basic meaning is **to receive** or **to become**.

> I <u>got</u> several presents for my birthday.
> I'll return to school after I <u>get</u> well.

Among its many other uses, **to get** is used to mean **to understand**, especially when talking about jokes or tricks.

> Everyone laughed loudly, but Maria just didn't <u>get it</u>.
> Say that again. I don't <u>get</u> your meaning.

A PHRASE JUST FOR FUN

MAN!

You certainly know the meaning of the word **man**; however, it is often used to show **surprise**, **excitement**, or **enthusiasm**. It can be used when speaking to a man, a woman, or a group, but remember that it is a **very casual** expression and rarely heard in formal speech.

> <u>Man</u>! I didn't even see that bus coming!
> Oh, <u>man</u>! Just think! Two more hours and vacation starts!
> <u>Man</u>, what a day! It's perfect for a picnic.

---

51. TO GET AT (SOMETHING)

This use of **to get** says that someone **is implying** something or **is trying to bring up a certain subject**.

> I don't know what you're talking about. What are you <u>getting at</u>?
> If you're trying <u>to get at</u> the reason for my anger, you're going to have to speak more kindly.

52. TO GET OVER SOMEONE/SOMETHING

This use of **to get** says that someone is **no longer interested** in another person or a thing. It usually also gives the idea that there **used to be great interest** and there was some difficulty in losing that interest.

> He's having a hard time <u>getting over</u> her. They dated for two years.
> I just can't <u>get over</u> Grandmother's death. I loved her so much.

53. THE GIFT OF GAB

Use this idiom when you want to say that someone is a **very talented speaker** or has the **ability to convince** others of what he or she believes.

> Anna has <u>the gift of gab</u>. She was able to talk the policeman out of the traffic ticket.
> You should be a car salesman. You really have <u>the gift of gab</u>.

54. ON THE GO

This phrase is usually used in place of **busy** and **in a hurry**.

> John is always rushing somewhere—to work, then to school, then home again. He's always <u>on the go</u>.
> Her busy job really keeps her <u>on the go</u>.

55. TO GO AGAINST ONE'S GRAIN

This strange combination of words means that someone or something is **annoying** or **irritating**.

> He talks too much. He really <u>goes against my grain</u>.
> Gossip and rumors always <u>went against her grain</u>.

56. TO GO TO THE DOGS

The meaning of this phrase actually has nothing to do with dogs. It is another way of saying that something **is in very bad shape** or **ruined**.

> During the depression, the whole country <u>went to the dogs</u>.
> If you keep acting like that, your reputation is going <u>to go to the dogs</u>.

57. WITH A GRAIN OF SALT

This phrase comes to English from an ancient source. It was originally used in Latin: *cum grano salis*. In English it means that someone **believes** something but is **skeptical** or **careful** in accepting the information given.

> The statements of the politician must sometimes be taken <u>with a grain of salt</u>.
> Jane has often lied. I take everything she says <u>with a grain of salt</u>.

58. TO GUESS SO

The verb **to guess** normally means that someone **draws a conclusion** or **makes presumptions** from certain information.

> If I had <u>to guess</u> your age, I'd say you are twenty.
> He <u>guessed</u> right. The book was hidden in a drawer.

But this verb is also used in place of **to think** or **to believe** or **to suppose**.

> Do you want to go shopping? I <u>guess so</u>.
> I <u>guess</u> Maria won't be going to school today. She's still sick.

59. TO LEND A HAND

This idiom is a synonym for **to help** or **to aid**.

> You seem busy. Can I <u>lend a hand</u>?
> Jane was always willing <u>to lend</u> her teachers <u>a hand</u>.

60. TO HAPPEN (TO KNOW/TO BE/TO DO)

The verb **to happen** means **to occur**.

> It <u>happened</u> on Friday night.
> What <u>happened</u> to you yesterday?

When followed by an infinitive phrase it means **by chance**.

> He <u>happened to be</u> at the same party.
> Do you <u>happen to know</u> where State Street is?

A PHRASE JUST FOR FUN

TO PAINT THE TOWN RED

This amusing phrase says that someone or some group of people went out for **a long evening of fun**. It also means that the fun-seekers probably had **too much to drink**.

> The night of graduation the whole class went down to Main Street to <u>paint the town red</u>.
> He was suffering from a hangover this morning because last night he <u>painted the town red</u>.

---

61. TO HITCHHIKE/HITCHHIKER/HITCHHIKING

This phrase describes **getting a free ride** in someone else's car. Hitchhikers usually stand at the side of a road, and wave their extended thumbs to passing cars as a signal that they need a **free ride**.

> Many people think <u>hitchhiking</u> is dangerous.
> My mother doesn't like me to <u>hitchhike</u> to school even though it saves a lot of money.
> I usually stop for <u>hitchhikers</u> if it's raining.

62. TO HOLD ONE'S TONGUE

This phrase is used in place of **to remain silent** or **not to speak**.

> <u>Hold your tongue</u>. Such language is disgraceful.
> Father told him <u>to hold his tongue</u>, but Jim continued to shout at him.

63. HOT AIR

This is a funny expression that means something said is probably **a lie** or **a terrible exaggeration**.

> He said he bought a new car, but I think he's full of <u>hot air</u>.
> She says she has a lot of boyfriends but it's all <u>hot air</u>.

64. TO BE IN HOT WATER

This is a synonym for **to be in trouble**.

> You broke Mom's vase. You're <u>in hot water</u> now!

65. HOW ABOUT?

This phrase should be used **to ask whether someone is interested in** doing something. Note that it is usually followed by a gerund (going, being, and so on) and is used in a question.

> <u>How about</u> going to a movie tonight?
> <u>How about</u> getting some lunch after the next class?

66. TO BE ILL AT EASE

This idiom says that someone **feels uncomfortable** in a particular situation, because that person **feels out of place** or **conspicuous**.

> You don't have <u>to be ill at ease</u> at the party. They're all very nice people.

67. TO JUMP TO CONCLUSIONS

This phrase means that someone is **making quick assumptions** about a person or situation without knowing all the facts.

> You always <u>jump to conclusions</u>. I didn't tear the drapes. The dog did it!

68. TO KEEP A STIFF UPPER LIP

This idiom means that someone **remains brave** throughout a difficult situation.

> <u>Keep a stiff upper lip</u>, Private. The battle will be won soon enough.

69. TO KEEP IN MIND

A simpler synonym for this phrase is **to remember**.

> <u>Keep in mind</u> that there'll be a test on this material tomorrow.
> Can't you <u>keep</u> this information <u>in mind</u> for just one day?

70. TO KEEP IN TOUCH (WITH)

This phrase means **to maintain communication** with someone whether by telephone, letter, or other means.

> After you move to New York, please <u>keep in touch</u>.
> I've <u>kept in touch</u> with my friends in Mexico for five years.

A PHRASE JUST FOR FUN

TO PULL SOMEONE'S LEG

This unusual phrase has nothing to do with the **physical pulling** of anyone's leg. It really means **to tease** someone or **to joke with** someone.

> He said he thought I could be a great musician, but when he laughed I knew he <u>was</u> just <u>pulling my leg</u>.
> She ran away with Jim? No! You're <u>pulling my leg</u>!

---

71. ON THE LEVEL

This phrase is a synonym for **honest**.

> You can always trust John. He's always <u>on the level</u>.
> <u>On the level</u>! I didn't do it!

72. TO BE LIABLE

Use this phrase when you want to say that **it is probable** that something will happen. Note that an infinitive usually follows this phrase.

> My sister <u>is liable</u> to say almost anything.
> It's <u>liable</u> to rain. You'd better take an umbrella.

73. TO LOOK FORWARD TO

This expression means that someone is **looking at the future with great expectation**.

> The young girl <u>was looking forward</u> **to** the big dance.
> I'll <u>be looking forward</u> **to** seeing you again.

74. LOOK OUT!

This idiom can stand alone as a brief sentence of warning **to be careful**.

> <u>Look out</u>! There's a bus coming!
> <u>Look out</u>! Don't fall!

75. TO LOSE ONE'S TEMPER

Use this expression when you want to say that someone **is becoming angry**. It suggests that the person's anger has developed **suddenly**.

> I hate it when Mom <u>loses her temper</u> and punishes us.
> James quickly <u>lost his temper</u> and began shouting at everyone.

76. TO HAVE A LUMP IN ONE'S THROAT

This phrase is used to say that someone feels **great sadness** or **emotion** that causes a tightness in the throat. Often, tears well up in the eyes at the same time.

> I read the last several pages of Anne Frank's diary with <u>a lump in my throat</u>.
> After the film he couldn't speak because he <u>had a lump in his throat</u>.

77. TO MAKE BELIEVE

This is a synonym for the verb **to pretend**.

> Let's <u>make believe</u> we're hunting in the jungle.
> The children like <u>to make believe</u>.

78. TO MAKE ONESELF AT HOME

Use this expression to say that you are **so comfortable** in someone else's home that you feel that you are almost **in your own home**.

> Take off your shoes and <u>make yourself at home</u>.
> They were so kind to me that they <u>made me feel</u> right <u>at home</u>.

79. TO MIND

This phrase means that someone **cares about** or **is not indifferent to** or does not **agree with** what another person wishes.

> I don't <u>mind</u>. Go to the movies, if you want.
> Do you <u>mind</u> if I sit here?

80. TO MAKE SOMEONE'S MOUTH WATER/ SOMEONE'S MOUTH WATERS

These expressions are used to say that someone suddenly feels **great hunger** or **is anticipating food** very eagerly.

The smell of the turkey roasting <u>made Tom's mouth water</u>.
I walked past the bakery with <u>my mouth watering</u>.

A PHRASE JUST FOR FUN

TO RAIN CATS AND DOGS

This expression has absolutely nothing to do with animals. Use it when you want to say that **it is raining very hard**.

I'm not going out there. It's <u>raining cats and dogs</u>!

---

81. IN THE NICK OF TIME

This idiom says that someone is doing something **at the best possible time** and that what that person is doing is in the form of a **rescue**.

The police arrived at the crime scene just <u>in the nick of time</u>.
Bill stopped her from falling <u>in the nick of time</u>.

82. TO PAY THROUGH THE NOSE

Use this funny little expression to say that someone is **paying far too much** for something.

They finally got the room they wanted, but they had <u>to pay through the nose</u> to get it.
You'll <u>pay through the nose</u>, if you go to that expensive store.

83. OR SO

Add this short expression after a number or quantity to show that the amount is **approximate**.

I arrived in Los Angeles <u>a year or so</u> ago.
Get me <u>a pound or so</u> of flour and a stick of butter.

84. OUT OF THE QUESTION

This phrase means that something being discussed **is already decided** and **impossible to be considered any further**.

> You want to go at this late hour? <u>Out of the question</u>, young man!
> I'm afraid a vacation in Florida is <u>out of the question</u> this year.

85. TO PASS AWAY

This is a synonym for **to die** and is used to speak about someone's death **more delicately**.

> Her grandfather <u>passed away</u> last month.
> I was shocked to hear that your sister <u>had passed away</u>.

86. TO PAY A CALL ON/TO PAY SOMEONE A CALL

These expressions mean that someone is **visiting** someone else.

> I was in the neighborhood so I <u>paid a call on</u> the Smiths.
> He often <u>paid us a call</u> without first phoning.

87. TO GIVE SOMEONE A PIECE OF ONE'S MIND

This phrase means that someone is **angry** and **telling what he or she thinks** about a certain matter.

> He won't be asking for money again. Grandmother <u>gave him a good piece of her mind</u> and threw him out.

88. TO POKE FUN AT/TO MAKE FUN OF

These two phrases are used as synonyms for **to ridicule** or **to tease**.

> Why must you <u>poke fun at</u> your little brother?
> The other children always <u>made fun of</u> the way she walked.

89. TO PULL ONESELF TOGETHER

Use this phrase to say that someone is **regaining control of himself** and is **correcting his or her previous behavior**.

> She cried for two hours but finally <u>pulled herself together</u> in time for school.

90. TO PUT ON AIRS

This phrase means that someone is **acting conceited** or **pretending to be far better than he really is**.

> When John drives his father's convertible, he always <u>puts on airs</u>.
> She <u>was putting on airs</u> at the party, but everyone knew she had no money.

SCATTERBRAINED

This expression suggests that someone is **completely disorganized** or **a poor thinker**.

> She'll never finish that project. She's too <u>scatterbrained</u>.
> I doubt that Tom and Jack can fix the car. They're both so <u>scatterbrained</u>.

---

91. TO PUT UP WITH

This is a synonym for **to endure**.

> Mother won't <u>put up with</u> the noise for much longer.
> I've <u>put up with</u> your lies for the last time!

92. RED TAPE

This expression is used to say that governments and other official institutions have **too many complicated procedures** or **too many difficult forms to be filled out** in order to use one of their services.

> All I want is a tax form—why all this <u>red tape</u>?
> The administrator's office kept us tied up in <u>red tape</u> for hours.

93. RIGHT AWAY

This is an adverbial expression that can be used as a replacement for **immediately**.

> I think you'd better get home <u>right away</u>. Mother is very sick.
> She said she wanted to return the gift <u>right away</u>.

94. TO KNOW THE ROPES

This phrase says that someone is **properly trained** and is **familiar with the procedures** of a particular job or task.

> Mary really <u>knows the ropes</u> around this office.
> You should help him. I don't think he <u>knows the ropes</u> yet.

95. TO RUN OUT OF

This expression is used to say that someone has **exhausted the supply** of a certain product or that **it is used up**.

> I think we're about <u>to run out of</u> milk.
> They <u>ran out of</u> gas just before getting to Chicago.

96. FROM SCRATCH

Use this prepositional phrase in place of **from the beginning**.

> I've lost count. I'd better start <u>from scratch</u>.

97. TO SEE EYE TO EYE

This phrase is used to mean that two people **agree** on something.

> I think we can sign the contract. I believe we <u>see eye to eye</u> on this matter.

98. TO SHOW OFF

This idiom means that someone is **acting in a way that makes a good impression** or is **acting in a way that makes his or her best characteristics apparent**.

> John <u>was showing off</u> to impress the others with his importance.
> Don't <u>show off</u>. It doesn't impress anyone!

99. TO BE SICK OF

This phrase means that someone finds something **unbearable** or can **no longer endure** it.

> She left him because she was <u>sick of</u> his constant complaining.
> Will the sun never shine? I'm <u>sick of</u> this weather!

100. TO SPEND (TIME)

You probably already know that the verb **to spend** is used to mean **to pay money**, but with expressions of **time** it means that someone is **passing time**. The expressions of time can be very brief or very long: a minute, an hour, three days, a vacation, and so on.

> We usually <u>spend</u> the winter in California.
> Why do we have <u>to spend</u> so many days with these people?

A PHRASE JUST FOR FUN

MANY HAPPY RETURNS OF THE DAY

This phrase is used primarily in the form given above. It is used as a form of **congratulations** for a special day such as a birthday, anniversary, or wedding.

> The man walked up to the bride and groom and said joyfully, "<u>Many happy returns of the day</u>!"

---

101. A STONE'S THROW

This is a synonym for **near** or **nearby**.

> Their house is just <u>a stone's throw</u> from ours.

102. A SWELLED HEAD

This unusual expression says that someone is **conceited** or **feeling over confident** about something.

> Don't flatter her. She already has <u>a swelled head</u>.
> I said nothing about his good looks. I didn't want to give him <u>a swelled head</u>.

103. TO TAKE AFTER

This phrase says that someone is **very similar** to another person or **looks like** another person—often a relative.

> With their red hair and green eyes, the children all <u>take after</u> their father.

104. ON THE TIP OF ONE'S TONGUE

This clever phrase can be used when you wish to say that you **almost remember** someone or something.

> I know your face, and your name is <u>on the tip of my tongue</u>.
> John stood silent before his teacher, although the answer was <u>on the tip of his tongue</u>.

105. TO HAVE A SWEET TOOTH

This phrase says that someone **enjoys sweet foods** such as candy or cake.

> Tom <u>has a sweet tooth</u>. He can't go past the bakery without stopping in to buy something.

106. TOPSY-TURVY

This is used to say that something or some place is **in a terrible state** or **very disorganized**.

> Mother entered my room and became angry when she saw that everything was <u>topsy-turvy</u>.

107. TO TWIST AROUND ONE'S LITTLE FINGER

Use this phrase to mean that someone (usually a girl) has another person (usually a boy) **under her complete influence.** The boy will probably do anything the girl asks.

> Poor Jack. Anna <u>has him twisted around her little finger</u>.
> They were very much in love, but Mother always <u>had Father twisted around her little finger</u>.

108. WELL OFF

This is a synonym for **rich** or **wealthy**.

> The Browns live in that big house over there. They're really quite <u>well off</u>.

109. WHAT ON EARTH?

Use this emphatic question to show **great surprise** or to express **deep-felt shock**.

> <u>What on earth</u>?" he asked in alarm. "What was that loud noise?
> <u>What on earth</u> do you think you're doing?

110. A (LITTLE) WHITE LIE

This idiom is used to make a **lie** seem **not quite so bad**. Rather than a **great lie** it's only a **small untruth**.

> Why was she so angry? It was only <u>a little white lie</u>.
> Saying that I am younger than I am was just <u>a white lie</u>.

A PHRASE JUST FOR FUN

TO BE BORN WITH A SILVER SPOON IN ONE'S MOUTH

This phrase is rather long, but it is used in place of much shorter ones: **born wealthy** or **born to a life of comfort**.

> What does she know about work? She was <u>born with a silver spoon in her mouth</u>.

MORE PHRASES JUST FOR FUN

SIX OF ONE AND HALF A DOZEN OF THE OTHER

This is another long phrase that replaces a simple idea. Use it to mean that **it's all the same** or **there is no difference**.

> I don't care if we go skiing or sledding. To me it's six of one and a half a dozen of the other.

STICK-IN-THE-MUD

This phrase can mean that you are **just no fun** or **not able to change from your serious nature**.

> Don't invite Bill. He's such a stick-in-the-mud.

THAT'S THE STRAW THAT BROKE THE CAMEL'S BACK/THAT'S THE LAST STRAW

These two phrases are quite similar. They are used to say that something was **the final problem** and that someone **no longer has any patience to endure** it.

> You want another hundred dollars? Well, that's the straw that broke the camel's back!
> She lost her purse again. That's the last straw! I simply won't buy her another.

TO TALK SOMEONE'S HEAD OFF

This phrase should be used when you wish to say that someone is **talking too much** to another person.

> John stood in the corner as the annoying woman talked his head off.
> Mary was embarrassed. Her husband had been talking Mrs. Smith's head off.

TO TICK (SOMEONE) OFF

This expression is very casual and indicates that someone is **angry**.

> If you say that again, you're going to tick me off.
> After the dog bit him, Dad became really ticked off.

TO WET ONE'S WHISTLE

This is an old expression that is still used very widely. It means **to have a drink** and often refers to alcoholic beverages.

> Let's stop at this bar and <u>wet our whistles</u>.
> What a hot day. I need <u>to wet my whistle</u>.

WHATEVER!

This is a rather up-to-date expression and is used **to end a conversation or a debate**. Its use suggests that the speaker is frustrated by the conversation and has no more patience with the other speaker.

> John: "You took my car and drove to the city, then you spent my
>   money to buy yourself a dinner."
> Mary: "<u>Whatever!</u>"

WHAT'S UP?

Use this simple question to ask in very broad terms what someone **is doing now** or **has planned for later**, or to question **why someone has summoned you**.

> Hi, Tom. You look rather busy. <u>What's up</u>?
> I hurried right over after I got your phone call. <u>What's up</u>?

TO TAKE FORTY WINKS

This is a synonym for **to take a nap**.

> I'm really tired. I need <u>to take forty winks</u>.

SECTION TWO

EXERCISES

See answers beginning on page 95.

1. Review the idiomatic meaning of "about," then complete each of the following sentences with an INFINITIVE PHRASE.

   EXAMPLE: He was about to leave for school.

   A. My mother was about _____.

   B. Class was about _____ but John was still at home asleep.

   C. Let me know when the doctor is about _____.

2. Write FOUR ORIGINAL SENTENCES with the idiom "about."

   A. _____

   B. _____

   C. _____

   D. _____

3. Fill in the blanks below with the correct form: ABROAD or TO TRAVEL ABROAD.

   A. My sister worked _____ during the summer.

   B. When we _____, we always spend time in Italy.

   C. I like _____ in the winter.

   D. Her parents spent several months _____ and returned home tanned and healthy.

   E. Maria hopes _____ next month.

4. Write TWO ORIGINAL SENTENCES with "abroad" and TWO with "to travel abroad."

   A. _____

   B. _____

   C. _____

   D. _____

5. Review the idiomatic meaning of "to be afraid," then complete each of the sentences below with TWO appropriate phrases.

    A. I'm afraid _____.

    B. I'm afraid _____.

    C. The young woman was afraid _____

    _____.

    D. The stern judge was afraid _____

    _____.

6. Using the sentence below, write FOUR QUESTIONS with the interrogatives given: "The doctor is afraid she can't help the patient."

    A. WHO _____?

    B. WHY _____?

    C. WHOM _____?

    D. WHAT _____?

7. Complete the sentences beginning with "suddenly" and "all of a sudden" with the same phrases.

    EXAMPLE: Suddenly <u>the door opened</u>.
    All of a sudden <u>the door opened</u>.

    A. Suddenly _____.

    All of a sudden _____.

    B. Suddenly _____.

    All of a sudden _____.

    C. Suddenly _____.

    All of a sudden _____.

    D. Suddenly _____.

    All of a sudden _____.

8. Write FOUR ORIGINAL SENTENCES with the phrase "all of a sudden."

    A. _____

    B. _____

    C. _____

    D. _____

9. Fill in the blank with an adjective and noun that make good sense.

    EXAMPLE: <u>The boring concert</u> is all over. Let's go home.

    A. _____ is all over. Let's go home.

    B. _____ is all over. Let's go home.

    C. _____ is all over. Let's go home.

    D. _____ is all over. Let's go home.

10. Using the sentence below, write FOUR QUESTIONS with the interrogatives given: "At ten o'clock John knew the long battle was finally all over."

    A. WHAT _____?

    B. WHEN _____?

    C. WHO _____?

    D. WHY _____?

11. Conjugate the verb "to be" correctly and write each sentence in the PRESENT TENSE and in the PAST TENSE.

    A. The elderly man TO BE not all there.

    _____

    _____

    B. They said his children TO BE not all there.

    _____

    _____

    C. The frightened nurse asked if she TO BE all there.

    _____

    _____

12. Complete the dialogues below with a response that uses the phrase "not all there."

    A. JOHN: Why is the old man laughing like that?

    _____

    B. DOCTOR: Tell me something about your aunt's condition.

    _____

    C. MARIA: It's very difficult for me to understand them.

    _____

    D. TEACHER: One of the boys was behaving very badly today.

    _____

13. Rewrite each of the sentences below in the TENSES shown.

    A. My aunt ANSWERS the doorbell.

        PAST _____

        PRESENT PERFECT_____

        FUTURE _____

    B. DOES he always ANSWER the phone on the first ring?

        PAST _____

        PRESENT PERFECT_____

        FUTURE _____

14. Using the sentence below, write FOUR QUESTIONS with the interrogatives given: "Yesterday grandmother was too sick to answer the phone."

    A. WHO _____?

    B. WHEN _____?

    C. WHY_____?

    D. WHAT_____?

15. Conjugate the verb "to be" in the TENSE and with the SUBJECTS given.

    A. TO BE aware of the serious problem with her health.

        PRESENT TENSE:

        YOU _____

        HE _____

        THE BOYS _____

        THEY_____

    B. TO BE NOT aware of her presence in the room.

        PAST TENSE:

        I _____

        YOU _____

        THE ROBBER _____

        SHE _____

        THEY_____

16. Rewrite the sentences below with the correct TENSE and FORM of the phrase "to be aware of."

   A. Bill didn't know about your problem.

   _____

   B. When I got home, I finally heard about the terrible storm.

   _____

   C. The teacher will eventually know about your cheating.

   _____

   D. How could the children possibly know about the accident?

   _____

17. Fill in each blank below with the phrase "to get on the ball" in the correct FORM and TENSE needed.

   A. Why can't you _____?

   B. At last night's game Jim finally _____.

   C. Try harder and _____!

   D. You won't _____ by being so lazy.

   E. Your brother finally _____, when he was fifteen years old.

18. Complete the dialogues below with a response using the phrase "to get on the ball." Show who is responding (father, teacher, son, and so on).

   A. THOMAS: I feel so tired and lazy all the time.

   _____

   B. COACH: She used to be the best on our soccer team.

   _____

   C. MOTHER: Roberto, are you still in bed?

   _____

   D. VICTOR: I can't believe they fired Martin. I wonder why.

   _____

19. Rewrite each of the following sentences in the TENSE given.

   A. The dog IS MAKING a beeline for the open gate.

   PAST _____

   PAST PERFECT _____

B. Tom MAKES a beeline for the stack of sandwiches.

PAST _____

PRESENT PERFECT_____

PAST PERFECT _____

FUTURE _____

C. DID he always MAKE a beeline for the prettiest girl?

PRESENT _____

PAST PERFECT _____

FUTURE _____

20. Write FOUR ORIGINAL SENTENCES with the phrase "to make a beeline."

A. _____

B. _____

C. _____

D. _____

21. Rewrite the following sentences replacing the NOUNS or PRONOUNS given where necessary.

A. I am speaking to you on behalf of _____.

YOUR UNCLE_____

THIS CLASS_____

ALL THE STUDENTS_____

MRS. BROWN _____

B. They all work on _____ behalf.

ROBERT _____

THE CHILDREN_____

I _____

YOU _____

WE _____

HE _____

THEY _____

SHE _____

22. Write FOUR ORIGINAL SENTENCES with the phrase "on behalf of" or "on someone's behalf."

    A. _____

    B. _____

    C. _____

    D. _____

23. Rewrite the sentence below with the SUBJECTS given and make any other necessary changes.

    "I bet my bottom dollar that he's behind that door."

    WE_____

    THEY_____

    THE WOMEN _____

    SHE _____

    HE _____

    THE DETECTIVE _____

24. Write FOUR ORIGINAL SENTENCES with the phrase "to bet one's bottom dollar."

    A. _____

    B. _____

    C. _____

    D. _____

25. Rewrite each of the sentences and place the word BETTER in the correct position to give the sentence the meaning that this is what one "should" do.

    EXAMPLE: John comes to school early.
             John BETTER come to school early.

    A. She works very hard at her job.

    _____

    B. We never do anything wrong.

    _____

    C. My friends have enough money for the rest of us.

    _____

D. You look in every drawer and every closet.

_____

E. Michael saves every cent he earns.

_____

F. They don't drive too far into the mountains.

_____

G. He doesn't prepare lunch as slowly as yesterday.

_____

26. Write FOUR ORIGINAL SENTENCES with the idiom "better."

    A. _____

    B. _____

    C. _____

    D. _____

27. Rewrite the sentences below with the idiom "blue" in the TENSES given.

    A. Anna doesn't feel blue anymore.

       PAST_____

       PRESENT PERFECT_____

       PAST PERFECT _____

       FUTURE _____

    B. He's feeling so blue.

       PAST_____

       PRESENT PERFECT_____

       PAST PERFECT _____

       FUTURE _____

    C. My sister feels blue over this.

       PAST _____

       PAST PERFECT _____

       FUTURE _____

28. Replace the phrase "to be sad" with the idiom "to feel blue" in each of the sentences below: Retain the same TENSE of the original sentence.

    A. Her parents were often sad at Christmastime.

    _____

    B. You shouldn't be so sad all the time.

    _____

    C. They won't be sad when they learn who's coming to visit.

    _____

    D. I've been so sad since my best friend moved away.

    _____

29. Rewrite the following sentences replacing the NOUNS or PRONOUNS given where necessary.

    A. I have a bone to pick with _____.

       YOU_____

       SHE _____

       YOUR BROTHER_____

       THEY_____

       HE _____

    B. She thought she had a bone to pick with _____.

       I _____

       JOHN_____

       HER FRIENDS_____

       WE_____

30. Write FOUR ORIGINAL SENTENCES with the phrase "to have a bone to pick with" someone.

    A. _____
    B. _____
    C. _____
    D. _____

31. Rewrite the sentences below in the TENSES given. Make any other necessary changes.

    A. She breaks down and cries loudly.

       PAST_____

       PRESENT PERFECT_____

       PAST PERFECT_____

       FUTURE _____

    B. The athlete doesn't want to break down in front of them.

       PAST _____

       PAST PERFECT_____

       FUTURE _____

32. Write FOUR ORIGINAL SENTENCES with the phrase "to break down."

    A. _____

    B. _____

    C. _____

    D. _____

33. Rewrite the sentences below in the TENSES given. Make any other necessary changes.

    A. She breaks the ice and speaks first.

       PAST_____

       PRESENT PERFECT_____

       PAST PERFECT_____

       FUTURE _____

    B. It's hard for me to break the ice first.

       PAST_____

       PRESENT PERFECT_____

       FUTURE _____

34. Using the sentence provided, write FOUR QUESTIONS with the interrogatives given:

    "Her friend didn't know how to break the ice and say hello."

    A. WHO _____?

    B. WHY _____?

C. WHAT_____?

D. WHOSE_____?

35. Rewrite the sentence below with the new SUBJECTS given.

"Her presence at the meeting was a breath of fresh air."

HE _____

THEY_____

MR. BROWN_____

THE MEN_____

THE GIRLS _____

YOU _____

WE_____

JAMES_____

36. Write FOUR ORIGINAL SENTENCES with the phrase "a breath of fresh air."

A. _____

B. _____

C. _____

D. _____

37. Rewrite the sentence below with the new SUBJECTS given. Make any other necessary changes.

"He muttered something under his breath."

SHE _____

I _____

JAMES_____

THE WOMEN _____

THEY_____

WE _____

YOU _____

38. Complete the dialogues below with a response using the phrase "under one's breath." Show who is responding (father, teacher, friend, and so on).

   A. UNCLE: I think I hear whispering out in the garden.

   _____

   B. MICHAEL: Can you hear what the girls are saying?

   _____

   C. LAURA: I think that boy is talking about us.

   _____

   D. MRS. SMITH: You'd better be careful what you say about Mr. Jones.

   _____

39. Rewrite the sentences below in the TENSES given. Make any other necessary changes.

   A. I brush up on my tennis skills.

   PAST _____

   PRESENT PERFECT_____

   PAST PERFECT_____

   FUTURE _____

   B. They have to brush up on their English grammar.

   PAST _____

   PRESENT PERFECT_____

   PAST PERFECT_____

   FUTURE _____

40. Replace the verb "to study" or "to practice" with the phrase "to brush up on" in the sentences below. Retain the same tense.

   A. Maria needs to study math.

   _____

   B. Those boys should practice their long shots.

   _____

   C. I will practice my Spanish later on.

   _____

   D. Have you already studied your multiplication tables?

   _____

41. Complete the sentences below with phrases that make good sense.

    EXAMPLE: John always butts into <u>our conversation</u>.

    "John always butts into _____"

    A. _____

    B. _____

    C. _____

    D. _____

    "Why do you butt into _____?"

    E. _____

    F. _____

    G. _____

    H. _____

42. Replace the verb "to interrupt" or "to question" with the phrase "to butt in/into" in the sentences below. Retain the same tense.

    A. Jack always interrupts our conversation.

    _____

    B. I wish you wouldn't question our business.

    _____

    C. She has always interrupted when I made a report.

    _____

    D. He won't be able to interrupt your discussion now.

    _____

43. Change each sentence below to a question, and begin it with "by the way." Retain the same tense.

    EXAMPLE: "Bob is sick." "By the way, is Bob sick?"

    A. They are anxious to come home.

    _____

    B. You saw them at the soccer game.

    _____

    C. She knows when the party is.

    _____

D. His family is building a pool in the backyard.

_____

E. You have studied for the history test.

_____

F. All the salespeople will receive awards at the dinner.

_____

44. Rewrite each sentence below as a question and retain the same TENSE as the original.

A. Your brother is always such a card.

_____

B. Uncle John was a card in college.

_____

C. Those boys thought they were such cards.

_____

D. He won't be a card his whole life.

_____

E. The men in this club think they're such cards.

_____

F. The old comedian really wasn't such a card.

_____

45. Fill in the blanks below with an AUXILIARY VERB that makes good sense. Choose your verbs from this list:

MUST	HAVE TO	NEED TO	WANT TO
CAN	SHOULD	OUGHT TO	

EXAMPLE: He **MUST** catch the next train for New York.

A. We _____ catch the bus for Los Angeles.

B. Where _____ I catch a cab quickly?

C. Tomorrow I _____ catch the morning train.

D. _____ you catch the earlier bus?

E. Anna _____ catch a plane for Chicago.

F. The commuters _____ always catch a bus on this corner.

46. Write FOUR ORIGINAL SENTENCES with the phrase "to catch" transportation.

    A. _____

    B. _____

    C. _____

    D. _____

47. Rewrite the sentences below in the TENSES given. Make any other necessary changes.

    A. He finally catches on.

    PAST _____

    PRESENT PERFECT _____

    PAST PERFECT _____

    FUTURE _____

    B. Don't the children ever catch on?

    PAST _____

    PRESENT PERFECT _____

    PAST PERFECT _____

    FUTURE _____

48. Complete the dialogues below with a response using the phrase "to catch on." Show who is responding (father, teacher, friend, and so on).

    A. JANE: Why is math so hard for you?

    _____

    B. PROFESSOR: Mr. Smith has a lot of trouble with word problems.

    _____

    C. MARIA: I laughed at his joke, but I didn't think it was funny.

    _____

    D. JOHN: I hope you're not going to tell another riddle.

    _____

49. Rewrite the sentences below in the simple past tense.

    A. Your son is a chip off the old block.

    _____

    B. Maria thinks that you're a chip off the old block.

    _____

    C. Why don't you call me a chip off the old block?

    _____

    D. Robert looks like Dad—a chip off the old block.

    _____

    E. Every one of his sons has his blue eyes—they are chips off the old block.

    _____

    F. I don't want to be a chip off the old block.

    _____

50. Rewrite the following sentence in the TENSES given.

    "Uncle Bill tells them another cock-and-bull story."

    PAST _____

    PRESENT PERFECT_____

    PAST PERFECT_____

    FUTURE_____

51. Write FOUR ORIGINAL SENTENCES with the phrase "a cock-and-bull story."

    A. _____

    B. _____

    C. _____

    D. _____

52. Complete each of the following sentences with any appropriate word or phrase.

    A. Your sister often comes across as _____.

    B. Why do you talk like that? You're coming across as _____

    _____.

    C. Bob came across as _____.

D. I don't want to come across as _____ .

E. _____ comes across as very smart, but he's really rather stupid.

F. _____ is coming across as quite a good dancer.

53. Using the sentence below, write FOUR QUESTIONS with the interrogatives given.

"Mr. Smith's younger daughter came across as something of a wallflower."

A. WHY_____?

B. WHOSE_____?

C. WHO _____?

D. WHAT _____?

54. Rewrite the following sentences in the TENSES given. Make any other necessary changes.

A. The patient comes to slowly.

PAST_____

PRESENT PERFECT_____

PAST PERFECT_____

FUTURE _____

B. The man in the coma is coming to gradually.

PAST_____

PRESENT PERFECT_____

PAST PERFECT_____

FUTURE _____

55. Write FOUR ORIGINAL SENTENCES with the phrase "to come to."

A. _____

B. _____

C. _____

D. _____

56. Rewrite the following sentence replacing the NOUNS or PRONOUNS given where necessary.

    "I came to know _____ at work."

    HE _____

    THIS GENTLEMAN _____

    THESE LADIES _____

    SHE _____

    THEY _____

    YOUR DAUGHTER _____

57. Using the sentence below, write FOUR QUESTIONS with the interrogatives given.

    "By the end of the evening the boy had come to know the girl quite well."

    A. WHO _____?

    B. WHOM _____?

    C. WHEN _____?

    D. HOW WELL _____?

58. Rewrite the following sentence in the TENSES given.

    "I simply can't cope with you anymore."

    PAST _____

    PRESENT PERFECT _____

    PAST PERFECT _____

    FUTURE _____

59. Rewrite the following sentence replacing the NOUNS or PRONOUNS given where necessary.

    "How can you cope with _____?"

    THAT MAN _____

    YOUR MONEY PROBLEMS _____

    I _____

    THEY _____

    SHE _____

    IT _____

60. Rewrite the sentences below changing the phrase "to cope with" to some other suitable phrase. Helpful words: TO PUT UP WITH, TO BEAR, TO ENDURE, TO STAND.

    EXAMPLE: I can't cope with the noise. (I can't put up with the noise.)

    A. I don't know how mother copes with father's drinking.

    _____

    B. When you're older you'll be able to cope with life's problems.

    _____

    C. Can you really cope with weather like this?

    _____

    D. I'm tired of coping with your bad behavior.

    _____

61. Replace the word "clear" with the phrase "cut-and-dried" in the sentences below. Retain the same tense.

    A. The answer to her question is clear.

    _____

    B. Why argue? It's clear what we have to do.

    _____

    C. It's not clear to me how we should react in this situation.

    _____

    D. I thought it was clear what your next move should be.

    _____

    E. The guest list is not clear to me.

    _____

    F. Helen won't even discuss it. It's all clear to her.

    _____

62. Rewrite the following sentences in the TENSES given.

    A. He's always cutting classes.

    PAST _____

    PRESENT PERFECT_____

    PAST PERFECT_____

    FUTURE _____

B. We usually cut our English class.

PAST _____

PRESENT PERFECT _____

PAST PERFECT _____

FUTURE _____

63. Write FOUR ORIGINAL SENTENCES with the phrase "to cut" classes.

A. _____

B. _____

C. _____

D. _____

64. Rewrite the following sentences replacing the NOUNS or PRONOUNS given where necessary.

A. I really liked dating _____.

THAT GIRL _____

SHE _____

THEY _____

YOUR BROTHERS _____

B. Do you still want to date _____?

I _____

MARIA _____

OTHER BOYS _____

WE _____

65. Write FOUR ORIGINAL SENTENCES with the idiom "to date."

A. _____

B. _____

C. _____

D. _____

66. Complete each of the following sentences with one of the following phrases: UP TO DATE or OUT OF DATE.

   A. What a great car. It's very_____.

   B. I like your hat. It's very_____.

   C. It looks strange. I think it's just _____.

   D. Why do you dance like that? It's very _____.

   E. Grandmother's clothes look awful. They're _____.

   F. This is the latest step. It's very_____.

67. Complete the dialogues below with a response using the phrase "to be up to date" or the phrase "to be out of date." Show who is responding (father, teacher, friend, and so on).

   A. LISA: Oh, what a beautiful skirt!

   _____

   B. JOHN: I can't believe Tom is wearing that kind of shirt.

   _____

   C. MRS. SMITH: Look at those two. I remember when we used to dance like that.

   _____

   D. THOMAS: What kind of shoes are those?

   _____

68. Rewrite the following sentence in the TENSES given.

   "The sound of the locomotive slowly dies away."

   PAST _____

   PRESENT PERFECT_____

   PAST PERFECT_____

   FUTURE_____

69. Write FOUR ORIGINAL SENTENCES with the phrase "to be dying away."

   A. _____

   B. _____

   C. _____

   D. _____

70. Rewrite the following sentences replacing the NOUNS or PRONOUNS given where necessary.

    A. I simply can't do without _____.

        YOU_____

        SHE_____

        THEY_____

        HIS LOVE_____

        LUXURIES _____

    B. In the war we did without _____.

        SOAP_____

        HOT WATER _____

        IT _____

71. Write FOUR ORIGINAL SENTENCES with the phrase "to do without."

    A. _____

    B. _____

    C. _____

    D. _____

72. Rewrite the following sentence with any FIVE COMPLETIONS that make good sense.

    "I wouldn't dream of _____."

        EXAMPLE: I wouldn't dream of hurting you.

    A. _____

    B. _____

    C. _____

    D. _____

    E. _____

73. Rewrite the following sentence in the TENSES given and change the SUBJECT of the sentence to the new PRONOUN given.

    "He has to eat his own words."

        EXAMPLE: PRESENT / She has to eat her own words."

    PAST / You _____

    PRESENT PERFECT / I _____

PAST PERFECT / We_____

FUTURE / They _____

74. Write FOUR ORIGINAL SENTENCES with the phrase "to eat one's own words."

A. _____

B. _____

C. _____

D. _____

75. Complete the following sentences with any appropriate phrase.

A. Please keep an eye on_____.

B. I had to keep an eye on_____.

C. She kept her eye on _____ all day.

D. Why did he have to keep an eye on_____?

E. Did Maria keep an eye on_____?

76. Using the sentence below, write FOUR QUESTIONS with the interrogatives given.

"Yesterday the babysitter had to keep an eye on four noisy children."

A. WHO _____?

B. ON WHOM _____?

C. WHEN _____?

D. HOW MANY _____?

77. Fill in each blank with any appropriate word or phrase.

A. The two leaders _____ face to face.

B. We finally were _____ face to face.

C. I hope someday to _____ you face to face.

D. She wants to _____ him face to face.

78. Using the sentence below, write FOUR QUESTIONS with the interrogatives given.

    "At the meeting the two enemies sat face to face for the first time."

    A. WHEN _____?

    B. WHERE _____?

    C. WHO _____?

    D. HOW MANY _____?

79. Rewrite the following sentences in the TENSES given and with the SUBJECTS given.

    A. He is falling in love.

       EXAMPLE: PRESENT / She is falling in love.

       PAST / We _____

       PRESENT PERFECT / They _____

       PAST PERFECT / You _____

       FUTURE / I _____

    B. He falls in love with San Francisco.

       PAST / I _____

       PRESENT PERFECT / We _____

       PAST PERFECT / She _____

       FUTURE / The tourists_____

80. Complete the dialogues below with a response using the phrase "to fall in love." Show who is responding (father, teacher, friend, and so on).

    A. BROTHER: You really don't know this boy very well.

       _____

    B. MOTHER: Is there something you want to tell me about Maria and you?

       _____

    C. BOY: It's finally spring again. I wonder why I feel so strange.

       _____

    D. GIRL: Is this a proposal? You want to marry me?

       _____

81. Replace the word "pregnant" with the phrase "in the family way." Retain the same tense.

   A. They're so excited—they're finally pregnant.

   _____

   B. Lydia felt fortunate to be pregnant again.

   _____

   C. You'll never guess who's pregnant!

   _____

   D. She's not pregnant. She just put on some weight.

   _____

   E. The newlyweds learned they're already pregnant.

   _____

   F. Being pregnant has made me a bit tired.

   _____

82. Rewrite the sentences below replacing the NOUNS or PRONOUNS given where necessary.

   A. I'm really fed up with _____.

   YOU _____

   TESTS _____

   THEIR GOSSIP _____

   THEY _____

   SHE _____

   B. Are they still fed up with _____?

   WE _____

   I _____

   HE _____

83. Write FOUR ORIGINAL SENTENCES with the phrase "to be fed up with."

   A. _____

   B. _____

   C. _____

   D. _____

84. Complete the following sentences with any appropriate phrases.

    A. Do you feel like _____ ?

    B. I don't feel like _____ today.

    C. Maria didn't feel like _____ .

    D. I really feel like _____ tomorrow.

    E. The students feel like _____ .

85. Using the sentence below, write FOUR QUESTIONS with the interrogatives given.

    "One of the friends probably won't feel like going fishing tomorrow."

    A. WHERE _____ ?

    B. WHEN _____ ?

    C. HOW MANY _____ ?

    D. WHY _____ ?

86. Rewrite the sentence below in the TENSES given. Note that this sentence is in the passive voice.

    "John is fired by the owner himself."

    PAST _____

    PRESENT PERFECT _____

    PAST PERFECT _____

    FUTURE _____

    FUTURE PERFECT _____

87. Write FOUR ORIGINAL SENTENCES with the phrase "to fire" someone.

    A. _____

    B. _____

    C. _____

    D. _____

88. Replace the word "strange" or "untrue" with the idiom "fishy." Retain the same tense.

   A. The boys' story sounded a bit strange.

   _____

   B. It's hard to believe you when you tell such a strange tale.

   _____

   C. Most of what she said was untrue.

   _____

   D. Don't tell us any more untrue stories about your life.

   _____

   E. The police found the thief's explanations strange.

   _____

   F. The young woman's actions looked rather strange.

   _____

89. Complete each sentence below with any appropriate phrases.

   A. After _____ he felt fit as a fiddle.

   B. _____ really looks fit as a fiddle.

   C. During _____ she looked fit as a fiddle.

   D. Since _____ he says he's been fit as a fiddle.

   E. Do _____ already feel fit as a fiddle?

90. Rewrite the sentences below changing the phrase "fit as a fiddle" to any other appropriate word or phrase.

   A. A few days after the operation she looked fit as a fiddle.

   _____

   B. I couldn't believe it. He was fit as a fiddle again.

   _____

   C. When you're finally fit as a fiddle, we'll take a long trip.

   _____

   D. Don't worry about me. I'm fit as a fiddle.

   _____

91. Fill in the blanks with an AUXILIARY VERB that makes good sense. Choose your verbs from this list:

MUST	HAVE TO	NEED TO	WANT TO
CAN	SHOULD	OUGHT TO	

EXAMPLE: He HAD TO foot the bill.

A. It's not fair that Father always _____ foot the bill.

B. But Uncle Fred never _____ foot the bill.

C. I don't have any money. I _____ foot the bill.

D. You _____ foot the bill at least once.

E. Grandfather already paid, so no one _____ foot the bill.

92. Using the sentence below, write FOUR QUESTIONS with the interrogatives given.

"At the party at the restaurant last week three guests had to foot the entire bill."

A. WHEN _____?

B. HOW MANY _____?

C. WHO _____?

D. WHERE _____?

93. Replace the verb "to understand" with the verb "to get" in the sentences below. Retain the same tense.

A. Barbara just didn't understand the joke.

_____

B. Don't try to understand his sense of humor.

_____

C. Everyone laughed, but Michael didn't seem to understand the story.

_____

D. No one was able to understand the humor in her words.

_____

E. I didn't understand the meaning of that comedy.

_____

F Even if you don't understand it, laugh anyway.

_____

94. Rewrite the following sentence replacing the NOUNS or PRONOUNS given where necessary.

    "What are you getting at?"

    SHE _____

    I _____

    THEY _____

    THE WOMEN _____

    HIS PROFESSOR _____

    HE _____

95. Fill in the blank in the following sentence replacing the NOUNS or PRONOUNS given where necessary.

    "It's time for you to get over _____."

    HE _____

    THIS _____

    YOUR ANGER _____

    THESE PROBLEMS _____

    THEY _____

    I _____

96. Complete the dialogues below with a response using the phrase "to get over." Show who is responding (father, teacher, friend, and so on).

    A. GIRLFRIEND: Sitting around and crying won't help. He's gone forever.

    _____

    B. SISTER: She left you long ago. You have to go on with your life.

    _____

    C. JUAN: I know how you feel. But mother died over a year ago.

    _____

    D. MOTHER: You survived the war, and you're home again.

    _____

97. Replace the phrase "to be a good speaker" with the phrase "to have the gift of gab" in each sentence below. Retain the same tense.

A. Juan was never a good speaker.

_____

B. If you're a good speaker, you can work in sales.

_____

C. Won't you ever be a good speaker?

_____

D. They listen intently, because the teacher is a good speaker.

_____

E. You have to be a good speaker to work here.

_____

F. How can you be a successful clerk without being a good speaker?

_____

98. Rewrite the following sentences in the TENSES given.

A. Jack is always on the go.

PAST _____

PRESENT PERFECT_____

FUTURE _____

B. His salespeople are on the go day and night.

PAST _____

PRESENT PERFECT_____

PAST PERFECT_____

FUTURE _____

99. Write FOUR ORIGINAL SENTENCES with the idiom "on the go."

A. _____

B. _____

C. _____

D. _____

100. Fill in the first blank with the SUBJECT given. Use the PRONOUN CUE given to fill in the second blank with the appropriate possessive adjective.

    "_____ really goes against _____ grain."

    EXAMPLE: THE NOISE/YOU—THE NOISE really goes against YOUR grain.

    A. HIS LANGUAGE/I— _____

    B. THAT/SHE— _____

    C. YOUR MUSIC/WE— _____

    D. SHOUTING/THEY— _____

    E. HER REMARKS/HE— _____

101. Write FOUR ORIGINAL SENTENCES with the phrase "to go against one's grain."

    A. _____

    B. _____

    C. _____

    D. _____

102. Rewrite the following sentences in the TENSES given.

    A. This town is going to the dogs.

        PAST _____

        PRESENT PERFECT_____

        PAST PERFECT_____

        FUTURE _____

    B. The former football star really went to the dogs.

        PRESENT PERFECT_____

        PAST PERFECT_____

        FUTURE _____

103. Rewrite the sentences below correctly using the phrase "to go to the dogs."

    A. This town is really in terrible shape.

    _____

    B. If he continues to drink like that, he'll end up ruined.

    _____

    C. Their old house is falling apart.

    _____

    D. After she lost all her money, she became an awful person.

    _____

104. Rewrite the sentences below as questions and begin each with the interrogative in BOLD LETTERS.

    A. WHO—The boys knew to take his story with a grain of salt.

    _____

    B. HOW—She accepted his explanation with a grain of salt.

    _____

    C. WHEN—They often took what he said with a grain of salt.

    _____

    D. HOW MANY—The two friends accepted one another's stories with a grain of salt.

    _____

    E. WHY—Tom was such a liar that she took his words with a grain of salt.

    _____

    F. WHOSE—The father accepted his son's tale with a grain of salt.

    _____

105. Write appropriate completions to each of the sentences below.

    A. I guess you think _____.

    B. I guess there will be _____.

    C. I guess we better _____.

    D. I guess she wants_____.

    E. I guess I have to _____.

    F. I guess the students ought to_____.

106. Fill in the blanks below replacing the NOUNS or PRONOUNS given where necessary.

    "Can I lend _____ a hand?"

    SHE _____

    YOU _____

    HE _____

    SOMEONE_____

    THEY_____

    THE FIREMEN _____

    THE BLIND MAN _____

107. Replace the verb in the sentence and "by chance" with the idiom "to happen to." Retain the same tense.

    A. Do you know by chance where Main Street is?

    _____

    B. He knew by chance that the buses didn't run on Sunday.

    _____

    C. Did Maria come to the party by chance?

    _____

    D. Will you by chance be going to the store later?

    _____

    E. By chance I have some spare change on me.

    _____

    F. By chance the guests arrived on time together.

    _____

108. Complete the sentence below with any appropriate word.

    "The student from Holland wanted to hitchhike to _____."

    A. _____

    B. _____

    C. _____

    D. _____

109. Using the sentence below, write FOUR QUESTIONS with the interrogatives given.

    "During a rainstorm he found it difficult to hitchhike home."

    A. WHERE _____ ?

    B. WHO _____ ?

    C. WHY _____ ?

    D. WHEN _____ ?

110. Rewrite the sentence below in the TENSES given.

    "I want to speak, but I hold my tongue."

    PAST _____

    PRESENT PERFECT _____

    PAST PERFECT _____

    FUTURE _____

111. Write FOUR ORIGINAL SENTENCES with the phrase "to hold one's tongue."

    A. _____

    B. _____

    C. _____

    D. _____

112. Using the sentence below, write FOUR QUESTIONS with the interrogatives given.

    "Many in the class believed these boys were full of hot air."

    A. WHO _____ ?

    B. HOW MANY _____ ?

    C. WHAT _____ ?

    D. WHY _____ ?

113. Rewrite the following sentence in the TENSES given.

    "You're really in hot water."

    PAST _____

    PRESENT PERFECT _____

    PAST PERFECT _____

    FUTURE _____

114. Complete the dialogues below with a response using the phrase "to be in hot water." Show who is responding (father, teacher, friend, and so on).

A. MARY: You shouldn't take the money without permission.

_____

B. THOMAS: You were out very late last night. And Dad knows about it.

_____

C. AUNT ANNA: Your behavior has been showing a lot of improvement.

_____

D. BROTHER: Mother found out you broke her favorite vase.

_____

115. Write four appropriate completions to the sentence below.

A. How about_____?

B. How about_____?

C. How about_____?

D. How about_____?

116. Rewrite the sentences below in the TENSES given.

A. I am always ill at ease when I'm with them.

PAST _____

PAST PERFECT_____

FUTURE _____

B. Do you feel ill at ease in this house?

PAST _____

PRESENT PERFECT_____

PAST PERFECT_____

FUTURE _____

117. Write FOUR ORIGINAL SENTENCES with the phrase "ill at ease."

A. _____

B. _____

C. _____

D. _____

118. Rewrite the following sentence in the TENSES given.

     "No matter what I say, he always jumps to conclusions."

     PAST _____

     PRESENT PERFECT_____

     PAST PERFECT_____

     FUTURE_____

119. Write FOUR ORIGINAL SENTENCES with the phrase "to jump to conclusions."

     A. _____

     B. _____

     C. _____

     D. _____

120. Fill in the blanks with an AUXILIARY VERB that makes good sense. Choose your verbs from this list:

MUST	HAVE TO	NEED TO	WANT TO
CAN	SHOULD	OUGHT TO	

     EXAMPLE: He HAD TO keep a stiff upper lip.

     A. I _____ you to keep a stiff upper lip.

     B. The boys really _____ keep a stiff upper lip.

     C. She just _____ not keep a stiff upper lip.

     D. Why _____ I keep a stiff upper lip?

     E. The wounded soldier _____ keep a stiff upper lip.

     F. He doesn't _____ keep a stiff upper lip.

121. Write FOUR ORIGINAL SENTENCES with the phrase "to keep a stiff upper lip."

     A. _____

     B. _____

     C. _____

     D. _____

122. Complete the sentence below replacing the NOUNS or PRONOUNS given where necessary.

"Just try to keep _____ in mind. That will help."

A. HE _____

B. SHE _____

C. WE _____

D. I _____

E. THEY _____

F. YOURSELF _____

G. OUR FAMILY _____

H. THE CHILDREN _____

123. Rewrite the sentences below replacing the NOUNS or PRONOUNS given where necessary.

A. I plan to keep in touch with _____.

YOU _____

THEY _____

ALL OF YOU _____

SHE _____

B. Mrs. Bennett never kept in touch with _____.

WE _____

I _____

HER RELATIVES _____

HE _____

124. Complete the dialogues below with a response using the phrase "to keep in touch with." Show who is responding (father, teacher, friend, and so on).

A. BEST FRIEND: I hope you'll write to me when you move to New York.

_____

B. FATHER: Why do you have to call her so often?

_____

C. ANNA: Promise you won't forget me.

_____

D. TEACHER: I know you'll like your new school and I hope you'll remember us here at your old school.

_____

125. Replace the word "honest" with the phrase "on the level" in each sentence below.

A. Honest! I saw it with my own eyes!

_____

B. His answers were always honest.

_____

C. Why does that lawyer think the robber's answers are honest?

_____

D. Just try to be honest with me, please.

_____

E. I don't want to talk to you if you can't be honest.

_____

F. Her explanation was honest but very hard to believe.

_____

126. Write five appropriate completions to the sentence below.

A. He's liable _____

B. He's liable _____

C. He's liable _____

D. He's liable _____

E. He's liable _____

127. Write FOUR ORIGINAL SENTENCES with the phrase "liable to."

A. _____

B. _____

C. _____

D. _____

128. Write five appropriate completions to the sentence below.

　　A. I'm really looking forward to_____

　　B. I'm really looking forward to_____

　　C. I'm really looking forward to_____

　　D. I'm really looking forward to_____

　　E. I'm really looking forward to_____

129. Using the sentence below, write FOUR QUESTIONS with the interrogatives given.

　　"Their three children were looking forward to visiting Disneyland next week."

　　A. HOW MANY _____?

　　B. TO WHAT_____?

　　C. WHEN _____?

　　D. WHOSE_____?

130. Write FOUR ORIGINAL SENTENCES with the warning "look out!"

　　A. _____

　　B. _____

　　C. _____

　　D. _____

131. Rewrite the sentence below in the TENSES given.

　　"Our teacher never loses his temper."

　　PAST _____

　　PRESENT PERFECT_____

　　PAST PERFECT_____

　　FUTURE_____

132. Complete the dialogues below with a response using the phrase "to lose one's temper." Show who is responding (father, teacher, friend, and so on).

　　A. JAMES: Why did you shout at Bill like that?

　　_____

　　B. SISTER: Father heard about your bad grades.

　　_____

C. COACH: You've got to learn not to fight during a game. Be a good sport.

_____

D. CLERK: The woman in Aisle Four is spanking her child.

_____

133. Complete the sentences below with any appropriate phrases.

"After _____ she had tears in her eyes and a lump in her throat."

A. After _____ she had tears in her eyes and a lump in her throat.

B. During _____ she had tears in her eyes and a lump in her throat.

C. Because of _____ she had tears in her eyes and a lump in her throat.

D. While at _____ she had tears in her eyes and a lump in her throat.

E. Coming from _____ she had tears in her eyes and a lump in her throat.

134. Using the sentence below, write FOUR QUESTIONS with the interrogatives given.

"After the funeral the mourners returned to their homes with a lump in their throats."

A. WHEN _____?

B. WHO _____?

C. WHERE _____?

D. WHAT _____?

135. Complete the sentences below with any appropriate phrases.

A. She always liked to make believe she _____.

B. Let's make believe we_____.

C. Did you ever make believe you_____?

D. The children were making believe_____.

E. Who made believe there was_____?

136. Write FOUR ORIGINAL SENTENCES with the phrase "to make believe."

    A. _____

    B. _____

    C. _____

    D. _____

137. Rewrite the sentence below replacing the NOUNS or PRONOUNS given where necessary, and make any other necessary changes.

    "I want BILL to make himself at home."

    EXAMPLE: HE—I want him to make himself at home.

    A. YOU _____

    B. SHE _____

    C. THE BOYS _____

    D. THEY _____

    E. EVERYONE _____

    F. MY GUEST_____

138. Complete the dialogues below with a response using the phrase "to make oneself at home." Show who is responding (father, teacher, friend, and so on).

    A. HOST AND HOSTESS: You shouldn't be nervous when you visit us.

    _____

    B. ROBERT: You'll feel very comfortable at my grandmother's house.

    _____

    C. GRANDMOTHER: I wish you wouldn't put your feet on that table.

    _____

    D. ANNA: Why are you sitting on the edge of your seat?

    _____

139. Complete the sentences below with any appropriate phrases.

    A. Do you mind if _____?

    B. Do you mind if _____?

    C. Do you mind if _____?

    D. I don't mind if _____.

140. Complete the following sentence six times with any appropriate phrases.

"_____ made his mouth water."

EXAMPLE: Smells from the kitchen made his mouth water.

A. _____

B. _____

C. _____

D. _____

E. _____

F. _____

141. Complete the following sentence six times with any appropriate phrases.

"_____ arrived just in the nick of time."

EXAMPLE: The ambulance arrived just in the nick of time.

A. _____

B. _____

C. _____

D. _____

E. _____

F. _____

142. Fill in the blanks below with an AUXILIARY VERB that makes good sense. Choose your verbs from this list:

MUST	HAVE TO	NEED TO	WANT TO
CAN	SHOULD	OUGHT TO	

EXAMPLE: He HAD TO pay through the nose.

A. John doesn't _____ pay through the nose.

B. No one _____ pay through the nose.

C. Why _____ Maria pay through the nose?

D. A stupid customer will _____ pay through the nose.

E. It was the last one. We _____ pay through the nose for it.

143. Using the sentence below, write FOUR QUESTIONS with the interrogatives given.

   "Because of their impatience the two brothers always paid through the nose."

   A. WHO _____?

   B. WHY _____?

   C. HOW MANY _____?

   D. WHEN _____?

144. Fill in the blanks with any appropriate phrases.

   A. It only cost _____ or so.

   B. They arrived in this country _____ or so ago.

   C. The movie lasted _____ or so.

   D. Anna's birthday was _____ or so ago.

   E. I think I can be at your house at _____ or so.

145. Write FOUR ORIGINAL SENTENCES with amounts and "or so."

   A. _____

   B. _____

   C. _____

   D. _____

146. Complete the sentence below with six appropriate phrases.

   "_____ is just out of the question."

   EXAMPLE: Working on Sunday is just out of the question.

   A. _____

   B. _____

   C. _____

   D. _____

   E. _____

   F. _____

147. Rewrite the sentences below in the TENSES given.

A. The old man passes away that day.

PAST _____

PRESENT PERFECT _____

PAST PERFECT _____

FUTURE _____

B. In the story she passes away exactly at noon.

PAST _____

PRESENT PERFECT _____

PAST PERFECT _____

FUTURE _____

148. Complete the sentence below replacing the NOUNS or PRONOUNS given where necessary.

"They often paid a call on _____."

A. WE _____

B. I _____

C. OUR FAMILY _____

D. THEIR FRIENDS _____

E. HE _____

F. SHE _____

149. Using the sentence below, write FOUR QUESTIONS with the interrogatives given.

"Every Sunday Grandfather paid a call on his relatives in the city."

A. WHO _____ ?

B. WHEN _____ ?

C. ON WHOM _____ ?

D. WHERE _____ ?

150. Complete the following sentences replacing the NOUNS or PRONOUNS given where necessary. Make any other necessary changes.

A. Mother gave _____ a piece of her mind.

HE _____

I _____

THEY _____

WE _____

THE CLERK _____

SHE _____

B. Father wants to give you a piece of his mind.

I _____

THEY _____

THAT ANGRY MAN _____

WE _____

EVERYONE _____

151. Replace the verb "to tease" or "to ridicule" with the phrase "to poke fun at" in the sentences below. Retain the same tense.

A. Why do you tease the little children so?

_____

B. I don't know why he ridicules her like that.

_____

C. If you continue to tease me, I'm going to scream!

_____

D. People shouldn't ridicule other people's problems.

_____

E. The sweet girl never teased anyone.

_____

F. The cruel boy ridiculed John mercilessly.

_____

152. Write THREE ORIGINAL SENTENCES with the phrase "to poke fun at" and THREE with the phrase "to make fun of."

A. _____

B. _____

C. _____

D. _____

E. _____

F. _____

153. Complete the following sentences replacing the NOUNS or PRONOUNS given where necessary. Make any other necessary changes.

   "He'd better pull himself together."

   EXAMPLE: ROBERT—Robert better pull himself together.

   A. YOU— _____

   B. THEY— _____

   C. TOM— _____

   D. HE— _____

   E. SHE— _____

   F. THE MOURNERS— _____

   G. THE WIDOW— _____

154. Complete the dialogues below with a response using the phrase "to pull oneself together." Show who is responding (father, teacher, friend, and so on).

   A. POLICE OFFICER: The poor woman sat on the curb and cried.

   _____

   B. THOMAS: My little brother couldn't get over losing his puppy.

   _____

   C. DOCTOR: You've been in the hospital for a week. Are you feeling better?

   _____

   D. PRIEST: Life must go on. You must get over your friend's death.

   _____

155. Fill in the blanks below with an AUXILIARY VERB that makes good sense. Choose your verbs from this list:

MUST	HAVE TO	NEED TO	WANT TO
CAN	SHOULD	OUGHT TO	

   EXAMPLE: He didn't HAVE TO put on airs.

   A. The girls really _____ not put on airs.

   B. Why do you _____ put on airs?

   C. Anyone _____ put on airs.

   D. I just don't _____ put on airs anymore.

   E. No one _____ put on airs.

156. Write FOUR ORIGINAL SENTENCES with the phrase "to put on airs."

   A. _____

   B. _____

   C. _____

   D. _____

157. Replace the verb "to endure" with the phrase "to put up with" in the sentences below. Retain the same tense.

   A. I don't think I can endure another minute here.

   _____

   B. No one should endure such language!

   _____

   C. I'm sorry, but I can't endure her chatter.

   _____

   D. Mrs. Brown couldn't endure her husband's stubbornness.

   _____

   E. I've endured it long enough. Now I'm through!

   _____

   F. Tom just won't endure any more fighting.

   _____

158. Write four appropriate completions to the sentence below.

   "When I went to _____ all I got was a lot of red tape."

   A. _____

   B. _____

   C. _____

   D. _____

159. Using the sentence below, write FOUR QUESTIONS with the interrogatives given.

   "He stood in line for hours and then got a lot of red tape."

   A. WHO _____?

   B. WHAT _____?

   C. HOW LONG_____?

   D. WHERE _____?

160. Replace the word "immediately" with the idiom "right away" in the sentences below.

    A. I expect a reply from you immediately.

    _____

    B. They went into the woods and found the dog immediately.

    _____

    C. You can't understand everything immediately.

    _____

    D. Aunt Helen immediately drove back home.

    _____

    E. They immediately understood the seriousness of the situation.

    _____

    F. I'll be there immediately.

    _____

161. Complete the following sentences replacing the NOUNS or PRONOUNS given where necessary. Make any other necessary changes.

    "You're fired! You just don't know the ropes!"

    A. HE _____

    B. THE NEW MAN _____

    C. SHE _____

    D. THE FOREMAN _____

    E. THEY _____

    F. THE APPRENTICES _____

162. Rewrite the sentences below with the phrase "to know the ropes."

    A. My uncle has worked here many years and is good at his job.

    _____

    B. You got fired because you just couldn't handle the work.

    _____

    C. She can't work here until she has more training.

    _____

    D. When you know something about this business, I have a job for you.

    _____

163. Complete the sentences below with any appropriate phrases.

    A. I'm afraid we've run out of _____.

    EXAMPLE: I'm afraid we've run out of <u>water</u>.

    _____

    _____

    _____

    _____

    B. Hurry! We're about to run out of _____.

    _____

    _____

    _____

    _____

164. Using the sentence below, write FOUR QUESTIONS with the interrogatives given.

    "It was immediately apparent that they would run out of water by sunset."

    A. WHAT _____?

    B. WHO _____?

    C. WHEN _____?

    D. WHY_____?

165. Replace the phrase "from the beginning" with the phrase "from scratch" in each sentence below.

    A. I don't get it. You'd better start from the beginning.

    _____

    B. There were so many mistakes in his work that he had to start from the beginning.

    _____

    C. Stop right now and start from the beginning.

    _____

    D. If you don't start from the beginning, I won't understand a thing.

    _____

    E. The little boy started his strange story from the beginning.

    _____

    F. We'll have to work from the beginning.

    _____

166. Rewrite the following sentences in the TENSES given.

   A. We never see eye to eye.

   PAST _____

   PRESENT PERFECT _____

   PAST PERFECT _____

   FUTURE _____

   B. Do you two ever see eye to eye?

   PAST _____

   PRESENT PERFECT _____

   PAST PERFECT _____

   FUTURE _____

167. Write FOUR ORIGINAL SENTENCES with the phrase "to see eye to eye."

   A. _____

   B. _____

   C. _____

   D. _____

168. Write the following sentence in the TENSES given.

   "He is showing off again."

   A. PAST _____

   B. PRESENT PERFECT _____

   C. PAST PERFECT _____

   D. FUTURE _____

   E. FUTURE PERFECT By that time,_____

169. Complete the dialogues below with a response using the phrase "to show off." Show who is responding (father, teacher, friend, and so on).

   A. BOY: Look at John. He's so conceited.

   _____

   B. GIRL: I think Juan is a fantastic dancer.

   _____

C. ROBERT: Look how far I can jump!

_____

D. MARIA: I scored two goals in yesterday's soccer game.

_____

170. Rewrite the following sentences replacing the NOUNS or PRONOUNS given where necessary.

"I'm really sick of _____."

A. THIS_____

B. HE _____

C. THEY_____

D. THEM _____

"She quickly grew sick of _____."

E. SHE _____

F. WE_____

G. THAT_____

H. EVERYTHING_____

171. Write FOUR ORIGINAL SENTENCES with the phrase "to be sick of."

A. _____

B. _____

C. _____

D. _____

172. Fill in the blanks below with any word or phrase that makes good sense.

EXAMPLE: I often spend <u>a few hours</u> at the library.

A. We spent _____ in Florida last year.

B. Where do you like to spend _____?

C. I wish we had spent _____ at the university.

D. I never spend more than _____ jogging.

E. The tourists hoped to spend at least _____ on the tour bus.

F. Sometimes I spend _____ just thinking.

173. Using the sentence below, write FOUR QUESTIONS with the interrogatives given.

    "Years later he spent several days with his friends in Mexico."

    A. WHERE _____?

    B. WHEN _____?

    C. WITH WHOM _____?

    D. HOW MANY _____?

174. Write four appropriate completions to the following sentence.

    "Our new house is just a stone's throw from _____."

    A. _____

    B. _____

    C. _____

    D. _____

175. Using the sentence below, write FOUR QUESTIONS with the interrogatives given.

    "Last month Tom's parents bought a large house just a stone's throw from the lake."

    A. WHOSE_____?

    B. WHAT _____?

    C. WHEN _____?

    D. WHO _____?

176. Replace the phrase "to be conceited" with the idiom "to have a swelled head" in each sentence below. Retain the same tense.

    A. We don't want him to be conceited.

    _____

    B. Mary's pretty but I think she's conceited.

    _____

    C. Michael will probably always be conceited.

    _____

    D. The girls knew the handsome boy was conceited.

    _____

E. No one should be conceited.

_____

F. As teenagers, the twins had been conceited.

_____

177. Rewrite the following sentence replacing with the NOUNS or PRONOUNS given where necessary.

A. I think that Thomas takes after _____.

YOU _____

I _____

WE _____

HE _____

HIS GRANDFATHER _____

THEY _____

B. Their daughter seems to take after _____.

AN AUNT _____

SHE _____

SOMEONE ELSE _____

THE GRANDPARENTS _____

178. Write FOUR ORIGINAL SENTENCES with the phrase "on the tip of one's tongue."

A. _____

B. _____

C. _____

D. _____

179. Rewrite the sentence below, filling in the blank with any appropriate word or phrase.

"John really likes _____. He has such a sweet tooth."

A. _____

B. _____

C. _____

D. _____

180. Replace the phrase "a mess" with the idiom "topsy-turvy" in each sentence below.

    A. This room is a mess!

    _____

    B. I walked into the class and saw that everything was a mess.

    _____

    C. How long is your bedroom going to remain a mess?

    _____

    D. Things were broken, there were papers everywhere, and the furniture was a mess.

    _____

    E. The neat stacks of documents were now a mess.

    _____

    F. Father's workshop was a mess again.

    _____

181. Write FOUR ORIGINAL SENTENCES with the phrase "to twist someone around one's little finger."

    A. _____
    B. _____
    C. _____
    D. _____

182. Rewrite the sentence below, filling in the blank with any appropriate word or phrase.

    "It's obvious they're well off. Just look at _____."

        EXAMPLE: It's obvious they're well off. Just look at their new car.

    A. _____
    B. _____
    C. _____
    D. _____

183. Rewrite each sentence below with the phrase "well off."

   A. His grandfather is a very rich man.

   _____

   B. I could tell by their house that they're rather wealthy.

   _____

   C. People say your family has a lot of money.

   _____

   D. Being rich doesn't always bring happiness.

   _____

184. Add the adjectives in BOLD LETTERS to the sentences below. Begin each line with the idiom "What on earth?"

   EXAMPLE: TALL—Who's that man?—
      What on earth? Who's that tall man?

   A. HORRIBLE   What's that noise?

   _____

   B. UGLY—How did that man get here?

   _____

   C. FOREIGN—When did his relatives arrive?

   _____

   D. ANGRY—What is all that shouting about?

   _____

   E. FOOLISH—Where did you hear such things?

   _____

   F. GIGANTIC—What is that creature?

   _____

185. Fill in the blanks below with an AUXILIARY VERB that makes good sense. Choose your verbs from this list:

MUST   HAVE TO   NEED TO   WANT TO
CAN   SHOULD   OUGHT TO

EXAMPLE: You MUST never even tell a white lie.

A. People _____ not tell little white lies to friends.

B. Nobody really _____ tell a white lie.

C. He _____ tell little white lies all day long.

D. In this case I thought I _____ tell a white lie.

E. Father says only a dishonest man _____ tell a white lie.

186. Write FOUR ORIGINAL SENTENCES with the phrase "a white lie."

A. _____

B. _____

C. _____

D. _____

SECTION THREE

TEST ONE

Idioms 1–10

A. *INSTRUCTIONS: Match the idiom to its definition by placing the LETTER of the idiom on the line next to the definition.*

(a) about
(b) abroad/to go abroad
(c) to be afraid
(d) all of a sudden
(e) all over

(f) not all there
(g) answer
(h) to be aware (of)
(I) to get on the ball
(j) to make a beeline for

_____ 1. to already know about something

_____ 2. to head directly toward somebody or some place

_____ 3. ready to begin some kind of activity

_____ 4. to need to improve one's skill or attitude

_____ 5. to hear a knock at the door and open it

_____ 6. unable to think clearly

_____ 7. an activity or event has ended

_____ 8. to regret that one cannot participate in something

_____ 9. to travel to another country

_____10. unexpectedly

B.   INSTRUCTIONS: *Complete each sentence below with a single word.*

1. Joe was about to _____ the phone, when mother picked up the receiver.

2. We're planning on traveling abroad. I hope to go to _____.

3. Martin is afraid that he _____ work with you tomorrow.

4. When the _____ is finally all over, we can go home.

5. The old woman wasn't all there and said such _____ things.

C.   INSTRUCTIONS: *Complete each sentence below with an appropriate phrase.*

1. All of a sudden _____.

2. I wasn't aware that _____.

3. Get on the ball! You're _____.

4. The frightened dog made a beeline for_____.

TEST TWO

Idioms 11–30

A. *INSTRUCTIONS: Match the idiom to its definition by placing the LETTER of the idiom on the line next to the definition.*

(a) on behalf of
(b) to bet one's bottom dollar
(c) better
(d) to be blue
(e) to have a bone to pick with
(f) to break down
(g) to break the ice
(h) a breath of fresh air
(i) under one's breath
(j) to brush up on

(k) to butt in
(l) by the way
(m) a card
(n) to catch
(o) to catch on
(p) chip off the old block
(q) cock-and-bull story
(r) to come across as
(s) to come to
(t) to come to know

_____ 1. to be depressed or sad

_____ 2. ought to do something

_____ 3. doing something for someone else

_____ 4. to become acquainted with someone

_____ 5. to awaken

_____ 6. something very unbelievable, perhaps a lie

_____ 7. in a whisper

_____ 8. to become very upset and cry

_____ 9. a welcome change

_____10. to be first to approach another person

_____11. not wanting to forget to mention something

_____12. to study something again

_____13. to interfere in a conversation or someone else's business

_____14. very much like one's father

_____15. to seem like

_____16. to be absolutely certain about something

_____17. to want to discuss a problem with someone

_____18. a funny, witty person

_____19. to understand a situation or a joke

_____20. to arrive in time to take transportation

B.   INSTRUCTIONS: *Complete the following sentences with a single word.*

1. On behalf of the _____ I want to thank our professors.

2. You'd better _____ a little money in the bank.

3. I have a bone to pick with _____.

4. You should be able to catch a _____ to the airport.

5. He was in a coma for a month but _____ came to this morning.

TEST THREE

Idioms 31–40

A. *INSTRUCTIONS: Match the idiom to its definition by placing the LETTER of the idiom on the line next to the definition.*

(a) to cope with
(b) cut-and-dried
(c) to cut a class
(d) to date
(e) to be up to/out of date

(f) to die away
(g) to do without
(h) one would not dream of it
(i) to eat one's own words
(j) to keep an eye on

_____ 1. to watch carefully, to guard

_____ 2. to handle a problem or situation with difficulty

_____ 3. to be wrong and have to admit it

_____ 4. absolutely clear

_____ 5. to be quite modern

_____ 6. to go out regularly with another person

_____ 7. to gradually become quieter and weaker

_____ 8. to intentionally miss a lesson

_____ 9. to have to be without someone or something

_____10. to be certain that someone would not do something

B. *INSTRUCTIONS: Complete each sentence below with a single word.*

1. This street is dangerous. Please keep an eye on my _____.

2. Those boys cut _____ yesterday.

3. Your _____ is rather out of date.

4. Tom and Anna have been dating since _____.

5. The sound of the _____ slowly died away.

C. *INSTRUCTIONS: Complete each sentence below with any appropriate phrase.*

1. Because he _____, he now has to eat his own words.

2. _____? I wouldn't dream of it!

3. During the storms we had to do without _____.

4. It's cut-and-dried that _____.

5. Our teacher has to cope with _____.

TEST FOUR

Idioms 41–60

A. *INSTRUCTIONS: Match the idiom to its definition by placing the LETTER of the idiom on the line next to the definition.*

(a) face to face
(b) to fall/to be in love
(c) in the family way
(d) to be fed up
(e) to feel like
(f) to fire
(g) fishy
(h) fit as a fiddle
(i) to foot the bill
(j) to get (something)

(k) to get at (something)
(l) to get over
(m) having the gift of gab
(n) on the go
(o) to go against one's grain
(p) to go to the dogs
(q) with a grain of salt
(r) to guess (so)
(s) to lend a hand
(t) to happen to

_____ 1. to imply something; to try to bring up a certain subject

_____ 2. to lose interest in something or someone

_____ 3. to be very annoying

_____ 4. being a talented speaker

_____ 5. to help someone

_____ 6. skeptically; with careful thought

_____ 7. looking directly at one another

_____ 8. to wish to do something

_____ 9. to develop a romantic relationship with someone

_____10. to discharge someone from a job

_____11. to understand a trick or a joke

_____12. to occur by chance

_____13. an idea or story that smells bad and doesn't seem right

_____14. in good health

_____15. to reluctantly have to pay

_____16. in a hurry and busy

_____17. to be in very bad shape

_____18. to believe; suppose

_____19. pregnant

_____20. to be completely annoyed with someone or something

B. *INSTRUCTIONS: Complete each sentence below with any appropriate phrase.*

1. We're so happy that _____ are in the family way.

2. I don't feel like _____ today.

3. We knew it was a fishy story when he said that _____.

4. He was nervous, because he was trying to get at _____.

5. _____ really goes against my grain.

TEST FIVE

Idioms 61–70

A. INSTRUCTIONS: *Match the idiom to its definition by placing the LETTER of the idiom on the line next to the definition.*

(a) to hitchhike
(b) to hold one's tongue
(c) hot air
(d) to be in hot water
(e) how about

(f) to be ill at ease
(g) to jump to conclusions
(h) to keep a stiff upper lip
(i) to keep in mind
(j) to keep in touch (with)

_____ 1. to remain brave

_____ 2. to remember

_____ 3. to feel uncomfortable in a certain situation

_____ 4. something that is probably a lie

_____ 5. asking whether someone is interested in doing something

_____ 6. to be in trouble

_____ 7. to make quick assumptions

_____ 8. to maintain communication with someone

_____ 9. to remain silent

_____10. get a free ride in someone else's car

B. INSTRUCTIONS: *Complete each sentence below with a single word.*

1. Hitchhiking in the desert can be _____.

2. She was in a lot of hot water because she _____.

3. During the _____ he tried to keep a stiff upper lip.

4. Can't you keep this _____ in mind for just one day?

5. She always kept in touch with her _____ in Europe.

C. INSTRUCTIONS: *Complete each sentence below with any appropriate phrase.*

1. I told him to hold his tongue, but _____.

2. He said that _____, but it was all hot air.

3. How about _____ tomorrow?

4. The poor children felt ill at ease at _____.

5. You always jump to conclusions, when _____.

TEST SIX

Idioms 71–90

A. *INSTRUCTIONS: Match the idiom to its definition by placing the LETTER of the idiom on the line next to the definition.*

(a) on the level
(b) to be liable
(c) to look forward to
(d) look out
(e) to lose one's temper
(f) to have a lump in one's throat
(g) to make believe
(h) to make oneself at home
(i) to mind
(j) to make someone's mouth water

(k) in the nick of time
(l) to pay through the nose
(m) or so
(n) out of the question
(o) to pass away
(p) to pay a call on
(q) to give a piece of one's mind
(r) to poke fun at
(s) to pull oneself together
(t) to put on airs

_____ 1. to angrily tell what one thinks

_____ 2. not possible to be considered any further

_____ 3. to visit

_____ 4. to die

_____ 5. an approximate amount

_____ 6. at the best possible moment

_____ 7. to have to spend too much money for something

_____ 8. to feel sadness or great emotion

_____ 9. to care, to not be indifferent

_____10. to pretend

_____11. to make oneself comfortable in a new situation

_____12. to cause someone to feel great hunger

_____13. honest

_____14. to become angry

_____15. to be probable that something will happen

_____16. warning to be careful

_____17. to have great expectations for the future

_____18. to act conceited

_____19. to regain control of oneself

_____20. to tease or ridicule

B.   INSTRUCTIONS: *Complete the sentences below with any appropriate phrase.*

1. Grandfather always lost his temper when _____.

2. Their children love making believe that _____.

3. Do you mind if _____?

4. _____ is simply out of the question.

5. He always puts on airs, but everyone knows that _____.

TEST SEVEN

Idioms 91–110

A. *INSTRUCTIONS: Match the idiom to its definition by placing the LETTER of the idiom on the line next to the definition.*

(a) to put up with
(b) red tape
(c) right away
(d) to know the ropes
(e) to run out of
(f) from scratch
(g) to see eye to eye

(h) to show off
(i) to be sick of
(j) to spend (time)

(k) a stone's throw
(l) having a swelled head
(m) to take after
(n) on the tip of one's tongue
(o) to have a sweet tooth
(p) topsy-turvy
(q) to have someone wrapped around one's finger
(r) well off
(s) what on earth?
(t) a (little) white lie

_____ 1. an untruth that isn't so bad

_____ 2. to be very similar to another person

_____ 3. expression showing great shock or surprise

_____ 4. overconfident or conceited

_____ 5. wealthy

_____ 6. nearby

_____ 7. to have to endure

_____ 8. to exhaust the supply of something

_____ 9. complicated and difficult governmental forms and procedures

_____ 10. to be properly trained

_____ 11. immediately

_____ 12. describing a girl, who has a boy under her complete influence

_____ 13. almost remembering something

_____ 14. in a terrible mess or state

_____ 15. to enjoy such sweets as candy, cakes, and cookies

_____ 16. to pass time

_____ 17. from the very start

_____ 18. no longer to be able to endure something

_____ 19. to agree on something with another person

_____ 20. to act in such a way as to make the best impression

B. INSTRUCTIONS: *Complete the sentences below with any appropriate phrase.*

1. Their teacher just can't put up with _____ anymore.

2. The new employee really knows the ropes concerning _____.

3. We'll never see eye to eye about how _____.

4. They say I take after _____.

5. Anna has a real sweet tooth. She often goes to the bakery and _____.

SECTION FOUR

ANSWER KEY FOR THE EXERCISES

NOTE: Sample answers have been provided for exercises where there is no single correct answer and an "individual student response" has been made.

1. Sample answers:
   A. sixteen when she learned how to drive.
   B. to begin.
   C. to leave.

2. Sample answers:
   A. The book is about 400 pages long.
   B. The teacher is about to begin.
   C. He is about forty years old.
   D. The story was about the Civil War.

3. A. abroad
   B. travel abroad
   C. traveling abroad
   D. abroad
   E. to travel abroad

4. Sample answers:
   A. He has gone abroad for six months.
   B. My friend is going to school abroad for a semester.
   C. My grandparents love to travel abroad.
   D. I dislike traveling abroad for longer than six weeks.

5. Sample answers:
   A. that I won't be able to go to your party.
   B. of scary stories.
   C. to walk alone at night.
   D. the defendant would break the law again.

6. A. Who is afraid she can't help the patient?
   B. Why is the doctor afraid she can't help the patient?
   C. Whom is the doctor afraid she can't help?
   D. What is the doctor afraid she can't do?

7. Sample answers:
   A. the doorbell rang.
   B. it began to rain.
   C. she began to scream.
   D. the boy began to cry.

8. Sample answers:
    A. He got up and left all of a sudden.
    B. All of a sudden it was quiet.
    C. The room filled up with people all of a sudden.
    D. All of a sudden the rain began to fall.

9. Sample answers:
    A. The snow storm
    B. The movie
    C. The party
    D. The dance

10. A. What did John know was finally all over?
    B. When did John know the long battle was finally all over?
    C. Who knew the long battle was finally all over?
    D. Why did John know the long battle was finally all over?

11. A. was
    B. were
    C. was

12. A. He's not all there.
    B. My aunt's not all there.
    C. They're not all there.
    D. I don't think he's all there.

13. A. answered, has answered, will answer
    B. did he always answer, has he always answered, will he always answer

14. A. Who was too sick to answer the phone?
    B. When was grandmother too sick to answer the phone?
    C. Why was grandmother too sick to answer the phone?
    D. What did grandmother do yesterday?

15. A. you are, he is, the boys are, they are
    B. I was, you were, the robber was, she was, they were

16. A. Bill wasn't aware of your problem.
    B. When I got home, I finally was aware of the terrible storm.
    C. The teacher will eventually be aware of your cheating.
    D. How could the children possibly be aware of the accident?

17. A. get on the ball
    B. got on the ball
    C. get on the ball
    D. get on the ball
    E. got on the ball

18. Sample answers:
    A. Father: You need to get on the ball.
    B. Teacher: Yes. She was really on the ball.
    C. Son: Yes. It's time to get up and get on the ball.
    D. Friend: His work was sloppy and he just wasn't on the ball.

19. A. was making, had been making
    B. made, has made, had made, will make
    C. does make, did make, will make

20. Sample answers:
    A. She made a beeline for the sales rack.
    B. The thirsty man made a beeline for the water fountain.
    C. I was so tired that I made a beeline for my bed as soon as I got home.
    D. We were hungry and made a beeline for the kitchen.

21. A. of your uncle, of this class, of all the students, of Mrs. Brown
    B. Robert's, the children's, my, your, our, his, their, her

22. Sample answers:
    A. He is acting on behalf of his friend.
    B. My mother answered the question on my behalf.
    C. The lawyer acted on his client's behalf.
    D. On behalf of everyone invited, thank you for a wonderful time.

23. WE bet our bottom dollar, THEY bet their bottom dollar, THE WOMEN bet their bottom dollar, SHE bet her bottom dollar, HE bet his bottom dollar, THE DETECTIVE bet his bottom dollar

24. Sample answers:
    A. I am so sure that I am correct that I'd bet my bottom dollar.
    B. He bet his bottom dollar on the race.
    C. Don't bet your bottom dollar if you are not sure that you will win.
    D. I bet my bottom dollar that my test answer was right.

25. A. she'd better work
    B. we'd better not do
    C. My friends better have
    D. You'd better look
    E. Michael better save
    F. They'd better not drive
    G. He'd better not prepare

26. Sample answers:
    A. You'd better get moving.
    B. I better get home now.
    C. If you are hungry, you'd better get something to eat.
    D. She'd better get to work soon.

27. A. didn't feel, hasn't felt, hadn't felt, won't feel
    B. was feeling, has been feeling, had been feeling, will be feeling
    C. felt, had felt, will feel

28. A. Her parents were often blue at Chirstmastime.
    B. You shouldn't be so blue all the time.
    C. They won't be blue when they learn who's coming to visit.
    D. I've been so blue since my best friend moved away.

29. A. with you, with her, with him, with them, with him
    B. with me, with him, with them, with us

30. Sample answers:
    A. I think we should talk. I have a bone to pick with you.
    B. After the nasty remark, she had a bone to pick with her boss.
    C. The man had a bone to pick with the person who pushed him.
    D. I have a bone to pick with whoever drank all the milk.

31. A. broke down and cried, has broken down and cried, had broken
    down and cried, will break down and cry
    B. didn't want, hadn't wanted, won't want

32. Sample answers:
    A. After the exhausting test, she broke down.
    B. This old car keeps breaking down.
    C. The man broke down after hearing the horrible news.
    D. I always break down at sad movies.

33. A. broke the ice and spoke, has broken the ice and spoken, had broken
    the ice and spoken, will break the ice and speak
    B. was hard, has been hard, will be hard

34. A. Who didn't know how to break the ice and say hello?
    B. Why didn't her friend know how to break the ice and say hello?
    C. What didn't her friend know how to do?
    D. Whose friend didn't know how to break the ice and say hello?

35. HIS presence, THEIR presence, MR. BROWN'S presence, THE MEN'S
    presence, THE GIRLS' presence, YOUR presence, OUR presence,
    JAMES' presence

36. Sample answers:
    A. Her smile was like a breath of fresh air.
    B. The rain was like a breath of fresh air after all that heat.
    C. The end of the long speech was like a breath of fresh air.
    D. Walking was like a breath of fresh air after sitting for six hours.

37. She muttered something under her breath. I muttered something under my breath. James muttered something under his breath. The women muttered something under their breath. They muttered something under their breath. We muttered something under our breath. You muttered something under your breath.

38. Sample answers:
    A. Nephew: Yes. I think Aunt Sue is whispering under her breath.
    B. Friend: No, they are whispering under their breath.
    C. Tom: I'm not sure. He is whispering under his breath.
    D. Mrs. Brown: I'd better whisper under my breath.

39. A. brushed, have brushed, had brushed, will brush
    B. had to brush, have had to brush, had had to brush, will have to brush

40. A. Maria needs to brush up on math.
    B. Those boys should brush up on their long shots.
    C. I will brush up on my Spanish later on.
    D. Have you already brushed up on your multiplication tables?

41. Sample answers:
    A. my business.
    B. your affairs.
    C. their conversations.
    D. our meetings.
    E. things that don't concern you?
    F. Tom's discussion?
    G. my friend's story?
    H. their plans?

42. A. Jack always butts into our conversation.
    B. I wish you wouldn't butt into our business.
    C. She has always butted in when I made a report.
    D. He won't be able to butt into your discussion now.

43. A. By the way, are they anxious to come home?
    B. By the way, did you see them at the soccer game?
    C. By the way, does she know when the party is?
    D. By the way, is his family building a pool in the backyard?
    E. By the way, have you studied for the history test?
    F. By the way, will all the salespeople receive awards at the dinner?

44. A. Is your brother always such a card?
    B. Was Uncle John a card in college?
    C. Did those boys think they were such cards?
    D. Will he be a card his whole life?
    E. Do the men in this club think they're such cards?
    F. Was the old comedian really such a card?

45.   Sample answers:
    A. need to
    B. can
    C. want to
    D. should
    E. must
    F. can

46.   Sample answers:
    A. I want to catch the next taxi.
    B. Tom caught a late train home.
    C. They are catching an earlier flight.
    D. We will catch the bus to work.

47.   A. He finally caught, He has finally caught, He had finally caught, He will finally catch
    B. Didn't the children ever catch on? Haven't the children ever caught on? Hadn't the children ever caught on? Won't the children ever catch on?

48.   Sample answers:
    A. Friend: I just can't catch on to division.
    B. Student: Some people just don't catch them.
    C. Tom: I didn't catch on to it either.
    D. Sue: Why? Didn't you catch the answer?

49.   A. Your son was a chip off the old block.
    B. Maria thought that you were a chip off the old block.
    C. Why did you call me a chip off the old block?
    D. Robert looked like Dad—a chip off the old block.
    E. Every one of his sons had blue eyes—they were chips off the old block.
    F. I didn't want to be a chip off the old block.

50.   told, has told, had told, will tell

51.   Sample answers:
    A. Tell the truth. I don't want another cock-and-bull story.
    B. I'm tired of all his cock-and-bull stories.
    C. What kind of cock-and-bull story is that?
    D. You can't believe that cock-and-bull story.

52.   Sample answers:
    A. silly
    B. rude
    C. unfriendly
    D. uncaring
    E. The man
    F. She

53. A. Why did Mr. Smith's daughter come across as something of a wall-flower?
    B. Whose daughter came across as something of a wallflower?
    C. Who came across as something of a wallflower?
    D. What did Mr. Smith's younger daughter do?

54. A. came to, has come to, had come to, will come to
    B. was coming to, has been coming to, had been coming to, will be coming to

55. Sample answers:
    A. The man took six hours to come to after his fall.
    B. After the phone rang, it took a few seconds for me to come to.
    C. He always needs his morning coffee to help him to come to.
    D. Some people need hours to come to after surgery.

56. him, him, them, her, them, her

57. A. Who had come to know the girl quite well by the end of the evening?
    B. Whom did the boy come to know quite well by the end of the evening?
    C. When did the boy come to know the girl quite well?
    D. How well did the boy come to know the girl by the end of the evening?

58. couldn't cope, haven't been able to cope, hadn't been able to cope, won't be able to cope

59. him, them, me, them, her, it

60. Sample answers:
    A. I don't know how mother puts up with father's drinking.
    B. When you're older you'll be able to bear life's problems.
    C. Can you really stand weather like this?
    D. I'm tired of putting up with your bad behavior.

61. A. The answer to her question is cut-and-dried.
    B. Why argue? It's cut-and-dried what we have to do.
    C. It's not cut-and-dried to me how we should react to this situation.
    D. I thought it was cut-and-dried what your next move should be.
    E. This guest list is not cut-and-dried to me.
    F. Helen won't even discuss it. It's all cut-and-dried to her.

62. A. was always cutting, has always been cutting, had always been cutting, will always be cutting
    B. cut, have cut, had cut, will cut

63.   Sample answers:
        A. Good students usually don't cut class often.
        B. I am going to cut science class today.
        C. He always cuts this class.
        D. I never cut Mr. Smith's class.

64.   A. her, her, them, them
        B. me, her, them, us

65.   Sample answers:
        A. I'm not dating anyone at the moment.
        B. She's been dating Tim for three weeks.
        C. Jim is too busy to date.
        D. Dating two people at the same time is hard work.

66.   A. up to date
        B. up to date
        C. out of date
        D. out of date
        E. out of date
        F. up to date

67.   Sample answers:
        A. Jill: Thanks. I try to keep my wardrobe up to date.
        B. Sue: I guess his fashion sense is a little out of date.
        C. Mr. Smith: I thought that dance was out of date.
        D. Annie: They're the most up to date designs from New York.

68.   died away, has died away, had died away, will die away

69.   Sample answers:
        A. My confusion died away as I thought a little harder.
        B. The rain stopped once the storm died away.
        C. The child's crying died away when his mother came home.
        D. Her anger over the waiter's insult has not died away yet.

70.   A. you, her, them, it, them
        B. it, it, it

71.   Sample answers:
        A. She is on a diet and does without snacks.
        B. In hard times, many people do without the extras.
        C. He is spoiled and could never learn to do without.
        D. To save money, I am doing without unnecessary shopping.

72. Sample answers:
    A. I wouldn't dream of leaving without you.
    B. I wouldn't dream of talking to that stranger.
    C. I wouldn't dream of stopping the party.
    D. I wouldn't dream of talking back to my teacher.

73. You had to eat your own words. I have had to eat my own words. We had had to eat our own words. They will have to eat their own words.

74. Sample answers:
    A. I was wrong. I'll have to eat my words.
    B. Even though she was wrong, she'll never eat her words.
    C. He's too proud to ever eat his words.
    D. Tom knew he was incorrect and had no problem eating his words.

75. Sample answers:
    A. the baby
    B. the telephone
    C. the children
    D. the neighbor's house

76. A. Who had to keep an eye on four noisy children yesterday?
    B. On whom did the babysitter have to keep an eye yesterday?
    C. When did the babysitter have to keep an eye on four noisy children?
    D. On how many children did the babysitter have to keep an eye yesterday? How many children did the babysitter have to keep an eye on yesterday?

77. A. met
    B. meeting
    C. meet
    D. meet

78. A. When did the two enemies sit face to face at the meeting?
    B. Where did the two enemies sit face to face for the first time?
    C. Who sat face to face at the meeting for the first time?
    D. How many enemies sat face to face at the meeting for the first time?

79. A. We were falling in love. They have been falling in love. You had been falling in love. I will be falling in love.
    B. I fell in love, We have fallen in love, She had fallen in love, The tourist will fall in love.

80. Sample answers:
    A. Sister: I know, but I have fallen in love with him.
    B Son: I think I'm falling in love with her.
    C. Girl: You've fallen in love, that's why.
    D. Boy: Yes. I fell in love with you the moment I saw you.

81. A. They're so excited—they're finally in the family way.
    B. Lydia felt fortunate to be in the family way again.
    C. You'll never guess who's in the family way!
    D. She's not in the family way. She just put on some weight.
    E. The newlyweds learned they're already in the family way.
    F. Being in the family way has made me a bit tired.

82. A. you, them, it, them, her
    B. us, me, him

83. Sample answers:
    A. I am fed up with my job.
    B. She's fed up with all your complaining.
    C. Mom is fed up with our fighting.
    D. The teacher was fed up with all the talking during class.

84. Sample answers:
    A. going to the movies
    B. working
    C. going out
    D. eating out
    E. reading

85. A. Where will one of the friends probably not feel like going tomorrow?
    B. When will one of the friends probably not feel like going fishing?
    C. How many friends will probably not feel like going fishing tomorrow?
    D. Why will one of the friends probably not feel like going fishing tomorrow?

86. was fired, has been fired, had been fired, will be fired, will have been fired

87. Sample answers:
    A. My boss was so mad that I thought he was going to fire someone.
    B. Jack was fired due to all his absences.
    C. No one has ever been fired from this company.
    D. Sooner or later, everyone gets fired.

88. A. The boy's story sounded a bit fishy.
    B. It's hard to believe you when you tell such a fishy tale.
    C. Most of what she said was fishy.
    D. Don't tell us any more fishy stories about your life.
    E. The police found the thief's explanations fishy.
    F. The young woman's actions looked rather fishy.

89. Sample answers:
    A. a good night's sleep
    B. The swim team
    C. her performance
    D. his operation
    E. you

90. Sample answers:
    A. A few days after the operation she looked as good as new.
    B. I couldn't believe it. He was healthy again.
    C. When you're finally well, we'll take a long trip.
    D. Don't worry about me. I'm in great physical condition.

91. Sample answers:
    A. has to
    B. wants to
    C. can't
    D. should
    E. needs to

92. A. When did three guests have to foot the entire bill at the party at the restaurant?
    B. How many guests had to foot the entire bill at the party at the restaurant last week?
    C. Who had to foot the entire bill at the party at the restaurant last week?
    D. Where did the three guests have to foot the entire bill last week?

93. A. Barbara just didn't get the joke.
    B. Don't try to get his sense of humor.
    C. Everyone laughed, but Michael didn't seem to get the story.
    D. No one was able to get the humor in her words.
    E. I didn't get the meaning of that comedy.
    F. Even if you don't get it, laugh anyway.

94. What is she getting at? What am I getting at? What are they getting at? What are the women getting at? What is his professor getting at? What is he getting at?

95. him, this, your anger, these problems, them, me

96. Sample answers:
    A. Sara: I know. It's time to get over him.
    B. Brother: But I still haven't gotten over her.
    C. Maria: I just can't get over her not being here.
    D. Son: I will never get over that experience.

97. A. Juan never had the gift of gab.
    B. If you have the gift of gab, you can work in sales.
    C. Won't you ever have the gift of gab?
    D. They listen intently, because the teacher has the gift of gab.
    E. You have to have the gift of gab to work here.
    F. How can you be a successful clerk without having the gift of gab?

98. A. was, has been, will be
    B. were, have been, had been, will be

99.   Sample answers:
       A. With my schedule, I'm always on the go.
       B. The kids keep her constantly on the go.
       C. Being on the go isn't always easy.
       D. You should be on the go more often.

100.   A. His language really goes against my grain.
       B. That really goes against her grain.
       C. Your music really goes against our grain.
       D. Shouting really goes against their grain.
       E. Her remarks really go against his grain.

101.   Sample answers:
       A. Telling lies really goes against my grain.
       B. The constant yelling really goes against my grain.
       C. Cheating goes against our teacher's grain.
       D. The child's crying went against the man's grain.

102.   A. was going, has been going, had been going, will be going
       B. has gone, had gone, will go

103.   A. This town is really going to the dogs.
       B. If he continues to drink like that he'll go to the dogs.
       C. Their old house is going to the dogs.
       D. After she lost all her money, she went to the dogs.

104.   A. Who knew to take his story with a grain of salt?
       B. How did she accept his explanation?
       C. When did they take what he said with a grain of salt?
       D. How many friends accepted one another's stories with a grain of salt?
       E. Why did she take his words with a grain of salt?
       F. Whose tale did the father accept with a grain of salt?

105.   Sample answers:
       A. you're right
       B. rain
       C. leave
       D. to stay
       E. study
       F. get to school

106.   her, you, him, someone, them, them, him

107.   A. Do you happen to know where Main Street is?
       B. He happened to know that the buses didn't run on Sunday.
       C. Did Maria happen to come to the party?
       D. Will you happen to be going to the store later?
       E. I happen to have some spare change on me.
       F. The guests happened to arrive on time together.

108.　Sample answers:
　　　A. school
　　　B. camp
　　　C. the park
　　　D. the beach

109.　A. Where did he find it difficult to hitchhike during a rainstorm?
　　　B. Who found it difficult to hitchhike home during a rainstorm?
　　　C. Why did he find it difficult to hitchhike home during a rainstorm?
　　　D. When did he find it difficult to hitchhike home?

110.　wanted to speak, but I held; have wanted to speak, but I have held; had wanted to speak, but had held; will want to speak, but I will hold

111.　Sample answers:
　　　A. Sometimes I get so angry and I can't hold my tongue.
　　　B. She should hold her tongue and not say such things.
　　　C. Mother held her tongue after the rude comment.
　　　D. He didn't hold his tongue and yelled at the man who shoved him.

112.　A. Who believed these boys were full of hot air?
　　　B. How many in the class believed these boys were full of hot air?
　　　C. What did many in the class believe?
　　　D. Why did many in the class believe these boys were full of hot air?

113.　were, have been, had been, will be

114.　Sample answers:
　　　A. Tom: When Father finds out I'm going to be in hot water.
　　　B. Sally: I'm going to be in hot water when he gets home.
　　　C. Nephew: I haven't been in hot water in weeks.
　　　D. Sister: I'm in hot water now.

115.　Sample answers:
　　　A. dinner
　　　B. going to the park
　　　C. some television
　　　D. a kiss

116.　A. I was always ill at ease when I was with him. I had always been ill at ease when I was with him. I will always be ill at ease when I'm with him.
　　　B. Did you feel ill at ease, Have you felt ill at ease, Had you felt ill at ease, Will you feel ill at ease

117. Sample answers:
      A. The shy boy was ill at ease in the crowded room.
      B. The nervous driver was ill at ease in all that traffic.
      C. I was ill at ease with his rude behavior.
      D. Mother was ill at ease when Tina didn't call as planned.

118. No matter what I said, he always jumped to conclusions. No matter
      what I have said, he always has jumped to conclusions. No matter what
      I had said, he had always jumped to conclusions. No matter what I will
      say, he will always jump to conclusions.

119. Sample answers:
      A. Don't jump to conclusions without knowing all the facts.
      B. A judge should not jump to conclusions without hearing all the
         evidence.
      C. Mother never jumps to conclusions. She always waits to hear my
         side of the story.
      D. I apologize for jumping to that conclusion.

120. Sample answers:
      A. need
      B. can
      C. should
      D. must
      E. wanted to
      F. have to

121. Sample answers:
      A. Men are expected to keep a stiff upper lip.
      B. Joe tried to keep a stiff upper lip at the funeral.
      C. She didn't keep a stiff upper lip after her boyfriend left her.
      D. I always keep a stiff upper lip, no matter how scared I am.

122. A. him
      B. her
      C. us
      D. me
      E. them
      F. yourself
      G. us
      H. them

123. A. you, them, all of you, her
      B. us, me, them, him

124. Sample answers:
     A. Jim: Of course! We'll always keep in touch.
     B. Daughter: I like keeping in touch with her.
     C. Dan: I will always keep in touch with you.
     D. Student: I'm going to keep in touch with all my old teachers.

125. A. On the level! I saw it with my own eyes!
     B. His answers were always on the level.
     C. Why does that lawyer think the robber's answers are on the level?
     D. Just try to be on the level with me, please.
     E. I don't want to talk to you if you can't be on the level.
     F. Her explanation was on the level but very hard to believe.

126. Sample answers:
     A. to yell
     B. to get angry
     C. hit somebody
     D. leave
     E. have an accident

127. Sample answers:
     A. I am liable to break something.
     B. She is liable to start crying.
     C. Tina is liable to throw the vase at him.
     D. Dan is liable to fall.

128. Sample answers:
     A. summer vacation
     B. my date tonight
     C. the baseball game
     D. going home
     E. her visit

129. A. How many children were looking forward to visiting Disneyland next week?
     B. To what were their three children looking forward next week?
     C. When were their three children looking forward to visiting Disneyland?
     D. Whose three children were looking forward to visiting Disneyland next week?

130. Sample answers:
     A. Look out for that dog!
     B. Look out! There's a bee in your hair.
     C. Look out for that car!
     D. Look out! He has a gun!

131.   lost, has lost, had lost, will lose

132.   Sample answers:
   A. Ellen: I just lost my temper.
   B. Brother: Did he lose his temper?
   C. Tina: I know I shouldn't lose my temper like that.
   D. Clerk: All that screaming must have made her lose her temper.

133.   Sample answers:
   A. the movie
   B. their discussion
   C. her sadness
   D. the wedding
   E. the funeral

134.   A. When did the mourners return to their homes with a lump in their throats?
   B. Who returned to their homes after the funeral with a lump in their throats?
   C. Where did the mourners return with a lump in their throats after the funeral?
   D. What did the mourners do after the funeral?

135.   Sample answers:
   A. was a princess
   B. are in space
   C. could fly
   D. they were invisible
   E. no cookies left

136.   Sample answers:
   A. I used to make believe I could fly.
   B. She made believe that she was an astronaut.
   C. The children made believe that they couldn't hear us.
   D. Mother made believe that there was no food for dinner.

137.   A. I want you to make yourself at home.
   B. I want her to make herself at home.
   C. I want the boys to make themselves at home.
   D. I want them to make themselves at home.
   E. I want everyone to make himself at home.
   F. I want my guest to make herself at home.

138.   Sample answers:
   A. Guest: I'll try to make myself at home.
   B. Sue: I'm sure I will be able to make myself at home.
   C. Grandson: I'm sorry. I guess I made myself at home too much.
   D. Joe: I just can't make myself at home.

139. Sample answers:
      A. I take one
      B. I go now
      C. I sit this dance out
      D. go to the movies

140. Sample answers:
      A. The thought of food
      B. The sight of the roasted turkey
      C. The freshly baked cookies
      D. The smell of apple pie
      E. The plate of fried chicken
      F. The pictures on the menu

141. Sample answers:
      A. The police
      B. The doctor
      C. The firemen
      D. The rescue workers
      E. The emergency supplies
      F. The Coast Guard

142. Sample answers:
      A. need to
      B. should
      C. must
      D. want to
      E. must

143. A. Who always paid through the nose because of their impatience?
      B. Why did the two brothers always pay through the nose?
      C. How many brothers always paid through the nose because of their impatience?
      D. When did the two brothers pay through the nose because of their impatience?

144. Sample answers:
      A. a dollar
      B. five months
      C. two hours
      D. a week
      E. seven

145. Sample answers:
      A. He arrived home an hour or so ago.
      B. Dinner will be at six or so.
      C. Mother will be here in a week or so.
      D. The cat was born four months or so ago.

146.   Sample answers:
    A. Cheating
    B. Lying
    C. Stealing
    D. Spanking the child
    E. Fighting
    F. Cursing

147.   A. passed away, has passed away, had passed away, will pass away
    B. passed away, has passed away, had passed away, will pass away

148.   A. us
    B. me
    C. our family
    D. their friends
    E. him
    F. her

149.   A. Who paid a call on his relatives in the city every Sunday?
    B. When did Grandfather pay a call on his relatives in the city?
    C. On whom did Grandfather pay a call in the city every Sunday?
    D. Where did Grandfather pay a call on his relatives every Sunday?

150.   A. him, me, them, us, him, her
    B. I want to give you a piece of my mind. They want to give you a piece of their mind. He wants to give you a piece of his mind. We want to give you a piece of our mind. Everyone wants to give you a piece of his mind.

151.   A. Why do you poke fun at the little children so?
    B. I don't know why he pokes fun at her like that.
    C. If you continue to poke fun at me, I'm going to scream!
    D. People shouldn't poke fun at other people's problems.
    E. The sweet girl never poked fun at anyone.
    F. The cruel boy poked fun at John mercilessly.

152.   Sample answers:
    A. You should not poke fun at your teacher.
    B. It's okay to poke fun at a good friend.
    C. Sally poked fun at John's haircut.
    D. Tom makes fun of everyone.
    E. We made fun of our reflections in the window.
    F. Mom made fun of Dad's slow walk into the kitchen.

153.   A. You'd better pull yourself together.
    B. They'd better pull themselves together.
    C. He better pull himself together.
    D. He'd better pull himself together.

E. She'd better pull herself together.

F. They better pull themselves together.

G. She better pull herself together.

154. Sample answers:

A. Man: She finally pulled herself together about an hour ago.

B. Sue: It will take a while for him to pull himself together.

C. Mr. Brown: I think I'm pulling myself together.

D. Tim: I'm trying to pull myself together.

155. Sample answers:

A. should

B. want to

C. can

D. need to

E. ought to

156. Sample answers:

A. I don't know why she has to put on airs.

B. She is tired of Jim always putting on airs.

C. You should never put on airs.

D. Father doesn't like when Frank puts on airs.

157. A. I don't think I can put up with another minute here.

B. No one should put up with such language!

C. I'm sorry, but I can't put up with her chatter.

D. Mrs. Brown couldn't put up with her husband's stubbornness.

E. I've put up with it long enough. Now I'm through!

F. Tom just won't put up with any more fighting.

158. Sample answers:

A. the billing department

B. the complaint desk

C. government office

D. tax bureau

159. A. Who stood in line for hours and then went through a lot of red tape?

B. What did he do for hours?

C. How long did he stand in line?

D. Where did he stand in line for hours and then go through a lot of red tape?

160. A. I expect a reply from you right away.

B. They went into the woods and found the dog right away.

C. You can't understand everything right away.

D. Aunt Helen drove back home right away.

E. They understood the seriousness of the situation right away.

F. I'll be there right away.

161. A. He's fired! He just doesn't know the ropes!
    B. The new man is fired! He just doesn't know the ropes!
    C. She's fired! She just doesn't know the ropes!
    D. The foreman is fired! He just doesn't know the ropes!
    E. They're fired! They just don't know the ropes!
    F. The apprentices are fired! They just don't know the ropes!

162. Sample answers:
    A. My uncle has worked here many years and knows the ropes.
    B. You got fired because you didn't know the ropes.
    C. She can't work here until she knows the ropes.
    D. When you know the ropes about this business, I have a job for you.

163. Sample answers:
    A. money, food, gas, stamps
    B. time, video tape, sunlight, candles

164. A. What was immediately apparent?
    B. Who would run out of water by sunset?
    C. When would they run out of water?
    D. Why would they run out of water by sunset?

165. A. I don't get it. You'd better start from scratch.
    B. There were so many mistakes in his work that he had to start from scratch.
    C. Stop right now and start from scratch.
    D. If you don't start from scratch, I won't understand a thing.
    E. The little boy started his strange story from scratch.
    F. We'll have to work from scratch.

166. A. saw, have seen, had seen, will see
    B. Did you two ever see, Have you two ever seen, Had you two ever seen, Will you two ever see

167. Sample answers:
    A. Even best friends don't always see eye to eye.
    B. I will never see eye to eye with him.
    C. Tom and Dan always see eye to eye on politics.
    D. We all see eye to eye on the type of decorations for the dance.

168. A. was showing off
    B. has been showing off
    C. had been showing off
    D. will be showing off
    E. By that time, he will have been showing off again.

169. Sample answers:
     A. Girl: Yes. He's a big show off.
     B. Boy: I think she's just a show off.
     C. Fred: Stop showing off.
     D. George: It sounds like you're showing off.

170. A. this
     B. him
     C. them
     D. his complaints
     E. her
     F. us
     G. that
     H. everything

171. Sample answers:
     A. I'm getting sick of her behavior.
     B. Ted is getting sick of Bill's lies.
     C. Sheila is sick of this bad weather.
     D. We were all sick of the loud noises.

172. Sample answers:
     A. two weeks
     B. the summer
     C. a few more days
     D. an hour
     E. six hours
     F. days

173. A. Where did he spend several days with his friends years later?
     B. When did he spend several days with friends in Mexico?
     C. With whom did he spend several days in Mexico years later?
     D. How many days did he spend with friends in Mexico years later?

174. Sample answers:
     A. the park
     B. here
     C. the lake
     D. your house

175. A. Whose parents bought a large house just a stone's throw from the lake last month?
     B. What did Tom's parents buy last month just a stone's throw from the lake?
     C. When did Tom's parents buy a large house just a stone's throw from the lake?
     D. Who bought a house last month just a stone's throw from the lake?

176. A. We don't want him to have a swelled head.
      B. Mary's pretty but I think she has a swelled head.
      C. Michael will probably always have a swelled head.
      D. The girls knew the handsome boy had a swelled head.
      E. No one should have a swelled head.
      F. As teenagers the twins had had a swelled head.

177. A. you, me, us, him, him, them
      B. her, her, someone else, them

178. Sample answers:
      A. His name is on the tip of my tongue.
      B. The answer was on the tip of my tongue but someone else responded first.
      C. Sue's telephone number is on the tip of my tongue.
      D. The name of the song we just heard is on the tip of my tongue.

179. Sample answers:
      A. chocolate
      B. cookies
      C. candy bars
      D. cake

180. A. This room is topsy-turvy!
      B. I walked into the class and saw that everything was topsy-turvy.
      C. How long is your bedroom going to remain topsy-turvy?
      D. Things were broken, there were papers everywhere, and the furniture was topsy-turvy.
      E. The neat stacks of documents were now topsy-turvy.
      F. Father's workshop was topsy-turvy again.

181. Sample answers:
      A. She has her boyfriend twisted around her little finger.
      B. The spoiled child has his parents twisted around his little finger.
      C. I'm too independent to ever be twisted around someone's little finger.
      D. Sue doesn't like the way Jim has Ellen twisted round his little finger.

182. Sample answers:
      A. their house
      B. their yacht
      C. their bank statement
      D. their private plane

183. A. His grandfather is very well off.
      B. I could tell by their house that they're rather well off.
      C. People say your family is well off.
      D. Being well off doesn't always bring happiness.

184. A. What on earth? What's that horrible noise?
      B. What on earth? How did that ugly man get here?
      C. What on earth? When did his foreign relatives arrive?
      D. What on earth? What is all that angry shouting about?
      E. What on earth? Where did you hear such foolish things?
      F. What on earth? What is that gigantic creature?

185. Sample answers:
      A. should
      B. ought to
      C. can
      D. needed to
      E. must

186. Sample answers:
      A. Sue told Bill a white lie to spare his feelings.
      B. Sometimes white lies are worse than total dishonesty.
      C. I would never tell a white lie to my best friend.
      D. Telling white lies should be kept to a minimum.

ANSWER KEY FOR THE TESTS

TEST ONE

A. 1-h, 2-j, 3-a, 4-I, 5-g, 6-f, 7-e, 8-c, 9-b, 10-d
B. Sample answers: 1. pick up, 2. London, 3. can't, 4. contest, 5. crazy
C. Sample answers: 1. there was a crash, 2. anyone was home, 3. late, 4. the house

TEST TWO

A. 1-d, 2-c, 3-a, 4-t, 5-s, 6-q, 7-i, 8-f, 9-h, 10-g, 11-l, 12-j, 13-k, 14-p, 15-r, 16-b, 17-e, 18-m, 19-o, 20-n
B. Sample answers: 1. graduating class, 2. put, 3. that rude lady, 4. bus, 5. finally

TEST THREE

A. 1-j, 2-a, 3-i, 4-b, 5-e, 6-d, 7-f, 8-c, 9-g, 10-h
B. Sample answers: 1. car, 2. class, 3. hair style, 4. last month, 5. explosion
C. Sample answers: 1. was wrong, 2. hit you, 3. watching television, 4. the only way to get there is to walk, 5. rude students

TEST FOUR

A. 1-k, 2-l, 3-o, 4-m, 5-s, 6-q, 7-a, 8-e, 9-b, 10-f, 11-j, 12-t, 13-g, 14-h, 15-i, 16-n, 17-p, 18-r, 19-c, 20-d

B. Sample answers: 1. you, 2. talking, 3. he won the race, 4. my reasons for being mad at him, 5. his nasty remark

TEST FIVE

A. 1-h, 2-i, 3-f, 4-c, 5-e, 6-d, 7-g, 8-j, 9-b, 10-a

B. Sample answers: 1. dangerous, 2. lied to her parents, 3. sad movie, 4. lesson, 5. aunt

C. Sample answers: 1. he yelled at the man anyway, 2. wasn't scared, 3. dinner, 4. the art museum, 5. it comes to my little brother

TEST SIX

A. 1-q, 2-n, 3-p, 4-o, 5-m, 6-k, 7-l, 8-f, 9-i, 10-g, 11-h, 12-j, 13-a, 14-e, 15-b, 16-d, 17-c, 18-t, 19-s, 20-r

B. Sample answers: 1. Sally put on airs, 2. they can fly, 3. cut ahead of you, 4. a European vacation, 5. he is a liar.

TEST SEVEN

A. 1-t, 2-m, 3-s, 4-l, 5-r, 6-k, 7-a, 8-e, 9-b, 10-d, 11-c, 12-q, 13-n, 14-p, 15-o, 16-j, 17-f, 18-i, 19-q, 20-h

B. Sample answers: 1. the constant talking, 2. this job, 3. to best solve the problem, 4. my uncle, 5. buys everything in sight

INDEX

The words are listed in alphabetical order. The number after the word indicates the page on which the word, with definition, first appears.

NOTES

NOTES

NOTES

BARRON'S POCKET GUIDES—

The handy, quick-reference tools that you can count on—no matter where you are!

A Pocket Guide
Synonyms

Quick help in finding different words with similar meanings. Includes list of 250 overused words. An aid to better writing style. Easy-to-use alphabetical format.

Arthur H. Bell, Ph.D.
Barron's Educational Series, Inc.

ISBN: 0-8120-4843-1
$7.95 Canada $10.50

BARRON'S
A POCKET GUIDE TO
Correct
English

Sentence construction
Spelling
Punctuation
Usage
Essays and letter writing
and more

Michael Temple

ISBN: 0-8120-9816-1
$6.95 Canada $8.95

BARRON'S
A POCKET GUIDE TO
Correct
Grammar
Third Edition

Parts of speech
Correct usage
Review of common grammatical errors and how to correct them

V. Hopper, C. Gale, and R. Foote
Revised by Benjamin W. Griffith

ISBN: 0-8120-9815-3
$6.95 Canada $8.95

BARRON'S
A POCKET GUIDE TO
Correct
Punctuation
Third Edition

Punctuation marks and how to use them
Emphasis on the logic of punctuation

Robert Brittain

ISBN: 0-8120-9814-5
$6.95 Canada $8.95

A Pocket Guide
Thesaurus

Quick help in finding alternate words with similar meanings and antonyms. Includes list of overused words. Easy-to-use alphabetical format.

Arthur H. Bell, Ph.D.
Barron's Educational Series, Inc.

ISBN: 0-8120-4845-8
$7.95 Canada $10.50

BARRON'S
A POCKET GUIDE TO
Correct
Spelling
Third Edition

28,000 often-misspelled words
Arranged alphabetically and divided into syllables
Easy-to-remember spelling rules

Francis Griffith

ISBN: 0-8120-9813-7
$6.95 Canada $8.95

BARRON'S
A POCKET GUIDE TO
Vocabulary
Third Edition

More than 3,000 words that appear on SAT and other standardized tests
Listed alphabetically with concise definitions and example sentences

Samuel Brownstein, Mitchel Weiner and Sharon Weiner Green

ISBN: 0-8120-9818-8
$6.95 Canada $8.95

BARRON'S
A POCKET GUIDE TO
Study
Tips
Fourth Edition

Tips for scheduling and organizing study time
How to take useful notes
How to correct your weak points

W. H. Armstrong, M. W. Lampe and G. Ehrenhaft

ISBN: 0-8120-9812-9
$6.95 Canada $8.95

BARRON'S
A POCKET GUIDE TO
Clichés

American clichés—their origins, their meanings, and examples used within the context of sentences
A useful supplement to English grammar texts and a valuable aid for ESL students

Arthur H. Bell

ISBN: 0-7641-0672-4
$6.95 Canada $9.50

Barron's EDUCATIONAL SERIES, INC.

250 Wireless Boulevard • Hauppauge, New York 11788
In Canada: Georgetown Book Warehouse
34 Armstrong Avenue • Georgetown, Ontario L7G 4R9
Visit our website at: www.barronseduc.com

Prices subject to change without notice. Books may be purchased at your bookstore, or by mail from Barron's. Enclose check or money order for total amount plus 15% for postage and handling (minimum charge $4.95). New York state residents add sales tax. All books are paperback editions.

(#18) R 9/98

BARRON'S BOOKS AND CASSETTES TO HELP YOU SUCCEED IN ESL AND TOEFL EXAMS

Where the Action Is: An Easy ESL Approach to Pure Regular Verbs
A clear, easy-to-follow guide complete with charts that instruct ESL students to use and understand pure regular verbs in speaking, reading and writing. Six practice test and answer keys are included. $7.95, Canada $10.50.

Barron's ESL Guide to American Business English
Focused to fit the needs of ESL students. Paperback handbook describes a variety of business writings and sample correspondence. Review section covers the basics of English grammar. $13.95, Canada $17.95.

Write English Right
A workbook with two cassettes presents exercises, assignment worksheets, and drills for TOEFL and ESL students. Accompanying cassettes feature oral exercises on English words that sound alike but have different meanings. $24.95, Canada $32.50. Book only $8.95, Canada $11.95.

American Accent Training
Concentrates on spoken English, American style, with exercises in American speech rhythms and inflections. Exercises prompt ESL students to listen and imitate, in order to be better understood by Americans, while also increasing listening comprehension. Package consists of book and three 90-minute cassettes in a durable case. $39.95, Canada $49.95.

Writing a Research Paper American Style: An ESL/EFL Handbook
Instructs advanced high school, college, and graduate students who have little experience in writing academic papers in English. Explains Modern Language Association and American Psychological Association rules, outlines documentation techniques, gives helpful grammar tips, and much more. $9.95, Canada $12.95.

Minimum Essentials of English
A concise 48-page summary of English grammar, rules, and language forms. An indispensable aid and style sheet to help with all written assignments. Pages are punched to fit a three-ring notebook binder. $6.95, Canada $8.95.

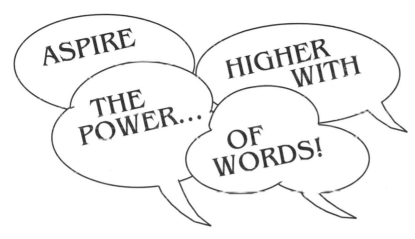

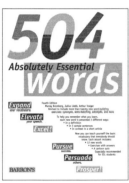
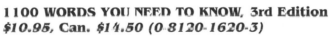

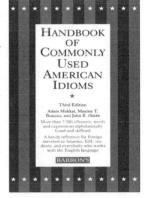

No One Can Build Your Writing Skills Better Than We Can...

Essentials of English, 4th Edition
$9.95, Can. $12.95 (0-8120-4378-2)
The comprehensive program for effective writing skills.

Essentials of Writing, 4th Edition
$9.95, Can. $12.95 (0-8120-4630-7)
A companion workbook for the material in *Essentials of English*.

10 Steps in Writing the Research Paper, 5th Edition
$9.95, Can. $12.95 (0-8120-1868-0)
The easy step-by-step guide for writing research papers. It includes a section on how to avoid plagiarism.

How to Write Themes and Term Papers, 3rd Edition
$10.95, Can. $14.50 (0-8120-4268-9)
The perfect, logical approach to handling theme projects.

The Art of Styling Sentences: 20 Patterns to Success, 3rd Edition
$8.95, Can. $11.95 (0-8120-1448-0)
How to write with flair, imagination and clarity, by imitating 20 sentence patterns and variations.

Writing The Easy Way, 2nd Edition
$12.95, Can. $16.95 (0-8120-4615-3)
The quick and convenient way to enhance writing skills.

Basic Word List, 3rd Edition
$6.95, Can. $8.95 (0-8120-9649-5)
More than 2,000 words that are found on the most recent major standardized tests are thoroughly reviewed.

BARRON'S EDUCATIONAL SERIES, INC.
250 Wireless Boulevard • Hauppauge, New York 11788
In Canada: Georgetown Book Warehouse
34 Armstrong Avenue • Georgetown, Ontario L7G 4R9
Visit our Website at: www.barronseduc.com